W9-CZA-321

READING AND WRITING IN THE ARTS - A handbook

BERNARD GOLDMAN
Wayne State University

Wayne State University Press
Detroit 1972

Copyright © 1972 by Wayne State University Press,
Detroit, Michigan 48202. All rights are reserved.
No part of this book may be reproduced without formal permission.

Published simultaneously in Canada
by The Copp Clark Publishing Company
517 Wellington Street, West
Toronto 2B, Canada.

Library of Congress Catalog Card Number: 73-165938
International Standard Book Number: 8143-1456-2

Library of Congress Cataloging in Publication Data

Goldman, Bernard, 1922–
Reading and writing in the arts.

1. Bibliography—Best books—Art. 2. Art—Bibliography. I. Title.
Z5931.G6 016.7 73-165938
ISBN 0-8143-1456-2

READING AND WRITING IN THE ARTS

Contents

1

Introduction

THIS handbook is intended primarily for the student beginning the study of the history of art and for the more advanced college major in art history. It is also planned as a handy, first-aid reference source for anyone interested in the several aspects of art and art history, for anyone who has a question relating to the visual arts but does not know where to seek the answer. Hence, the handbook provides references that tell how to identify saints in paintings and how to pack paintings for shipping, where to find the names of patrons of miniaturists and where to find the prices paid for such works, what is the relationship between artistic creativity and narcotics, how to prepare an article to submit to a journal, and what are the career opportunities in the fine arts.

Beginning students in a special field are faced with the troublesome and time-consuming task of locating the basic library resources that will provide information. Too often students are discouraged from learning some of the basic facts about a subject by the exasperating task of finding reference material; more often, they simply are not aware of the existence of a great variety of easily obtainable source material. There are college courses in bibliography and research techniques, but they are a rarity in art history curriculums. This handbook is not a substitute for a study of art history bibliography, but it serves the same purpose. It can reduce the frustration of not knowing where to look for information and can encourage students to locate the basic facts upon which art history studies are built. It is the answer to the plea time and again directed at librarians, art teachers, and historians of art: "Where can I quickly find out in art . . . .?"

The handbook is not a bibliography of art books in the several areas of art history, but is rather a guide to the books that will lead students to the scholarly material in an area of special interest. Hence, it is, in part, a bibliography of bibliographies, as well as a bibliography of basic source books. Because library research and report writing are an integral part of the study of art history, the handbook also contains a generalized description of research writing, which stresses ways to organize research rather than on specific styles of writing, subjects to study, or types of material to be researched.

Teachers of art and art history frequently assume that students sent off to libraries and museums to write papers have somewhere learned how to mine information, how to organize their research activities, how to document works of art and findings, how to evaluate published works, and, finally, how to write down their findings in a manner consistent with the demands of art history scholarship. Some value may accrue from forcing the student to find out for himself how to handle research work by trial and error, where to go for information, how to retrieve material, and how to organize and express his ideas. But the danger of this procedure, putting to one side the needless waste of time, is that the student is liable to give up out of sheer frustration, or that he becomes so involved in the mechanics of bibliographical control and reference-finding that the goal of research—discovery, clarification, and new understanding—is lost in the tangle of the means to get there. How often has the teacher found his brightest students more worried about the proper form for a footnote than about the reason for having it?

It is impossible to anticipate every type of reference material that art history students may need, just as it is impractical to list every reference tool available to them. This handbook attempts to organize the major source and reference works which are most commonly used in the study of art and which are the easiest for students to handle. A handbook such as this does not aim at completeness, but it should provide the reference tools that will lead the interested student to exhaustive material.

Included are references to much literature which technically is not cataloged as art history, but it is vital material in the study of art history, which is only one aspect of the broader areas of cultural history. Students need ready access to information related to, if not properly part of, art works and their history: myths and legends, stories of saints and heroes, biographies of the great, explanations of the symbols and the structures of religions. In addition, they frequently have questions concerning technical, factual matters that are part of the business of art production and maintenance: the techniques of the different media, the identification of forgery and alteration, the problems of conservation, the methods of photographing and printing works of art, the sources of reproductions and filmed material.

Indeed, it is not only the art history student who asks these questions, but also those whose contact with the arts is more casual. Art historians and librarians are constantly queried on small, but important practical matters that are ancillary to art history: how to find the name of an art dealer in Cologne; how to clean an oil painting at home; where to obtain a color reproduction of a favorite painting; where to find out which monuments and museums are located in a city to be visited; where to find biographies of Negro artists; where to find, if such exists, a dictionary of Irish artists (there is a two-volume book devoted to this matter). The professional historian, after years of experience, knows where to find answers to such questions; the reference librarian has an occupational interest in knowing how to locate the books that will give the desired information. But in the absence of these human sources, the student and layman can use this handbook as a reasonable substitute.

The student of art history who is planning on, or just beginning, a professional career in the arts will find that the information on publishing practices of scholarly journals will be of use as he prepares to make his own contributions to the field.

Several self-imposed limitations have guided the composition of this handbook, and I must note them to safeguard the reader from misusing the book or mistaking it for what it is not.

This handbook is not a full bibliography of reference works in the arts, nor a list of basic books, nor a complete compilation of bibliographies on the vast literature of art and art history. The volume could be increased tenfold in length and still not cover the most vital books available to research scholars. The objective of the handbook is to provide sufficient material for the student without offering so much that using the handbook itself would become a complicated, mysterious operation. My overriding concern is to simplify the locating of material by offering a selection of source books rather than to complicate it by a bewildering presentation of alternate choices in all languages and degrees of availability. (As a cautionary guide, I have kept in mind the old story of the child who was given a full dissertation on the reproductive organs when all he wanted to know was whether he was born at home or in a hospital.)

The problem of selection in composing the handbook has not been what to include, but rather what to exclude. The standards of selection used are simple in theory, although difficult to carry out. Admittedly, they imply a degree of personal judgment, based upon my experience in teaching, writing, and research, upon my habits of reading, and upon my preference in authors. Most difficult, perhaps, was my deletion of many favorite reference tools on the basis that they are not sufficiently useful in the types of research undertaken by students.

The first standard of selection is that the citation should be authoritative and offer specific information in brief, easily accessible form. When a choice is possible, preference is given to materials that also provide bibliographies or notes which lead the reader, should he so desire, to works of greater depth and detail. Some reference works have been included which do not fulfill this criterion, but only because they are useful in some other respect, sufficient to offset their shortcoming, or because there is no better source book. The annotations for each item note the virtues and vices of the book.

Second, I believe that the reader is best served by literature written in his own language. Even the most valuable reference work in art history is of small use to the student if he cannot read the language in which it is written. Even if the student can read a little German, French, or Italian, it is still preferable to provide him with an alternate English source where it is at all comparable to the foreign language book. But the history of art is international and for a long time was almost the exclusive preserve of European scholars. Hence, much of the most valuable reference material is available only in French or German. Foreign language books have been rigorously excluded in preference to English language books if the latter are comparable or nearly so. Exceptions have been made where nothing remotely as good exists in English. Perhaps these several inclusions will remind the student that there can be no serious study of the history of art without foreign language training.

The third standard of selection is that of availability. A reference citation is valuable to a student only if he can obtain it. Most students and general readers for whom this handbook is intended will not have access to the world's great art history library collections, of which there are a scant handful. Most American libraries of modest size will have few of the art history reference works, no matter how important, that were printed more than seventy-five years ago. Such venerable references have been almost completely excluded, except in cases in which reprints have been published recently. Also, the extremely costly, very rare, limited editions have been excluded because they are usually not available locally. I have always given preference to the more recent publications, to those that most likely can be found in college libraries and the larger public libraries. Where possible, alternate references are given, not in an attempt to be definitive, but in the hope that at least one of the cited sources will be available to the student. Graduate students who have at their command the resources of a major reference library in art history can quickly go beyond this guide.

The final standard of selection is that of subject popularity. All areas of art history are not equally popular in American college curriculums and with students. While it would be laudable to proselytize for the inclusion in our college studies of many areas of art that have been seriously neglected, such noble service is beyond the purpose of this handbook. Thus, I have given greater emphasis to references in those areas of art history which undergraduate students and laymen most frequently explore; I have devoted less space to periods and areas exotic to beginning studies.

It is evident, then, that the decisions on what has been included and what omitted will not completely satisfy any reader. Conversely, while the selections do reflect a personal element, they are not idiosyncratic. In the long run, the test of the selection process is not whether the results satisfy the teacher, but whether they are useful to his students.

For more comprehensive coverage of bibliographical materials in art history, I refer the student to two standard English language guides: Mary W. Chamberlin's *Guide to Art Reference Books* and E. Louise Lucas's *The Harvard List of Books on Art.* Both are excellent for the advanced student and librarian, although they are too inclusive to serve the purposes of the audience for which this handbook is intended. At the other end of the scale are some beginners' guides to the literature of art and art history—such as Neville Carrick's *How to Find Out about the Arts*—which well serve the needs of the general librarian for a broad introduction, but are not designed, and are not extensive enough, for the American college student.

The handbook is not intended to be read from cover to cover. As a tool to provide quick access to reference material in answer to specific questions, it should be consulted primarily through the index. The index has been cross-listed as broadly as possible, the range of headings covering both the technical, "correct" terms and phrases and those in popular use, in the hope of reducing the amount of guessing necessary to discover under what name or title the object of one's search can be found. Many of the niceties of bibliographical reference citation have been deliberately put to one side to keep each reference as short and succinct as possible. Thus, the citations do not recapitulate the publishing history of a volume (number of printings, editions, revisions, translators, successive editors, volumes, etc.). The citation is sufficient to get the student to any one of the possibly many editions of the book which his library may hold. (The year of the edition given in a citation, where more than one edition was printed, is that one which I had available for examination and is not necessarily the latest published.)

The section in the handbook on techniques of research, documentation, and writing also reflects my preferences to a certain extent. There is no single acceptable manner of research and writing. The handbook provides some suggestions that the student can adopt and adapt to his particular needs and inclinations. In general, the principles recommended are those commonly found in the professional literature of art history. Attention is given only to those matters of research and writing that are of particular or unique interest to the study of art history. General recommendations for reading and writing can be found in most basic English handbooks.

Magazines and journals in the arts range from those which publish crucial scholarly discoveries to those which specialize in gossip about art and artists. Usually the quality of articles can be estimated on the basis of the reputation of the journal, and the most responsible periodicals are listed here. In addition, I have included some of the popular magazines that report primarily on the current art scene; while limited in usefulness as source material for serious study, they are interesting for their current news reporting.

The practices of scholarly publication in journals have been briefly touched on for two reasons. First, advanced students and those just entering the professional field frequently express curiosity over the practical business of submitting articles to journals. Can anyone submit a book review for publication? Do journals publish only articles written by their sponsoring society's members? Does one need special permission to publish a photograph? Are journal editors omniscient, vindictive, and/or dilatory? What should the disappointed writer of a rejected article do? The section on writing for publication addresses itself to these and other related matters. Also, some understanding of the publishing practices in a scholarly field is useful to the student in helping him to evaluate what he reads. He must recognize, for example, that all printed material does not represent absolute truth. Too often the printed word is considered, by the fact of its being, the last word, and it is assumed that the editorial decision to publish is engendered by the divine and nurtured in the ideal. Very practical, matter-of-fact considerations, such as financial ones, have a strong influence on what is published and how it is published (there can be no question, for example, that it is more expensive to publish a long article than a short one). What is said here about journal publication is, by extension, largely true about noncommercial book publishing houses (those, such as university presses, whose primary consideration is not the financial return promised by a prospective book).

A final word: omission of a book or journal from this handbook does not mean that the student should avoid that particular source, that it is of dubious value or specious quality. The omission is probably the result of the selection practices described above, it may be the result of its having been published too recently for inclusion, or it is possible, alas, that it is the result of the author's innocence. (Students, teachers, and librarians interested in the present condition of bibliographical resources in the history of art should read the brief sketch of the subject by the head librarian of the Metropolitan Museum of Art: J. Humphry, III, "Architecture and the Fine Arts," in R. B. Downs and F. B. Jenkins, *Bibliography, Current State and Future Trends* (Urbana, 1967), pp. 142–57.)

The student always should consult the index first to find the reference sources. Each entry in the index is followed by one or more reference numbers (a prefix letter followed by digits). These reference numbers refer to the items in the bibliographical section of this handbook, not to the pages. The bibliography is divided into broad categories which are designated by the prefix letters. For example, the prefix "A" refers to the category of *A*rtists' biographical material, and the prefix "H" refers to the category of *H*istory of art books. The references are arranged in numerically sequential order throughout; the prefix letters merely alert the user of the index that he is being referred to a bibliography ("B"), a reference aid ("R"), or a journal or periodical ("J"), etc.

2

Reference Key by Subject

3

Bibliographical References and Source Materials

ART HISTORY BIBLIOGRAPHIES

This section lists the major bibliographies on art and art history, as well as some bibliographies that carry a section on the arts. Some specialized art history bibliographies are included—bibliographies of different media, different countries, etc.—to indicate the types of more specialized bibliographies that can be found for local and regional interests in the arts. A full listing of regional bibliographies, by country, can be found in Chamberlin (B-1).

B-1 Chamberlin, M. W. *Guide to Art Reference Books.* Chicago, 1959.

This is the most comprehensive basic English reference guide to books in the history of art. More than 2,500 entries include indexes, directories of artists and art works, dictionaries, encyclopedias, handbooks, periodicals, and some of the most important works in each of the several areas of the arts. An excellent index makes the book easy to use. Each entry contains a brief description of the contents of the citation, frequently with some evaluations, such as "old but still useful," or "colored plates leave much to be desired." Source materials in the several languages are included. Useful for both basic and advanced research, the book's only drawback for the undergraduate student or beginner in art history is that the contents are too complete. The student inexperienced in bibliographical resources may find the seemingly endless variety of possible references confusing because he is not in a position to evaluate which materials will be most practical for him to follow up at his level of study and, also, which can be found in his library.

B-2 Lucas, E. L. *The Harvard List of Books on Art.* Cambridge, 1952.
Not as comprehensive as Chamberlin (B-1), it presents a selected list of basic books under the categories of iconography, symbolism, architecture, sculpture, painting, drawing, graphic arts and illumination, and minor arts. Included are an alphabetical list of books on individual artists and an index of artists and authors cited. Its publication date indicates that it does not contain books published since 1952.

B-3 Lucas, E. L. *Art Books: a Basic Bibliography on the Fine Arts.* New York, 1968.
Based on the preceding volume by the same author (B-2), this book is designed to provide the basic list of books in the area of art history to be acquired by an undergraduate college library.

B-4 Carrick, N. *How to Find Out About the Arts.* Oxford, 1965.
A brief, basic selection of books on and about the arts, as well as the tools and materials available for art history research. Useful for students, its greatest value is probably to the apprentice librarian.

B-5 Dove, J. *Fine Arts.* London, 1966.
A somewhat too brief bibliography of books on art of the Western world, post antique. It also covers dictionaries, encyclopedias, and periodicals. Intended for use in England, it strongly emphasizes books on the arts of that land while omitting references to works of comparable importance in and on the arts in the United States.

B-6 Lueders, E., ed. *The College and Adult Reading List of Books in Literature and the Fine Arts.* New York, 1962.
The section on art lists books for the adult or college reader who is unfamiliar with the field. Described and evaluated are basic readings in architecture, painting, sculpture, design, crafts, graphics, art criticism, esthetics, and art reference books.

B-7 Young, A. R., ed. *Art Bibliography.* New York, 1941.
Considerably outdated now, but also quite hit-and-miss, the

bibliography gives some basic titles and some specialized articles.

B-8 Besterman, T. *A World Bibliography of Bibliographies.* Lausanne, 1965.
A librarian's basic guide, it contains a section on art history books (published through 1963) under the listing *Art,* columns 519–52. Included are bibliographies of periodicals, books on the history of the fine arts, of the decorative and applied arts, of art sales, and of bibliographies of art books by country. There is also a listing of catalogs of books in various libraries and collections.

B-9 Walford, A. J., ed. *Guide to Reference Material.* London, 1959, supplement, 1963.
Although intended for general library use in all areas, the book contains a section on the arts worth consulting for a brief, highly selected listing that emphasizes British materials, frequently to the exclusion of comparable works of other countries. The short evaluations and criticisms of almost every item are helpful.

B-10 Winchell, C. M. *Guide to Reference Books.* Chicago, 1967.
Intended for the librarian, the work describes general reference tools. It is useful in art history for both the art section, which is uneven in its selection, and for the reference citations in allied areas, such as folklore, mythology, history, and religion, with which research in art history must deal. Some 7,500 works of reference are listed.

B-11 *Worldwide Art Book Bibliographies (Syllabus).* New York.
Pamphlet-sized issues are published twice a year, by Worldwide Books, Inc. (New York), of "a select list of in-print books on the history of art and archaeology" from prehistory to the twentieth century. While not pretending to completeness, the current nature of the running publication makes the listing useful in keeping track of new publications and in building library holdings.

B-12 *Annuario bibliografico di storia dell'arte, Instituto nazionale d'archeologia e storia dell'arte.* Modena, 1954—.

An annual bibliography of art with listings by artists, countries, including short annotations and synopses (in Italian). It is very handy as an international listing and is indexed by authors and artists referred to in the citations.

B-13 *Répertoire d'art et d'archéologie* and *Bibliographie d'histoire de l'art.*
Both bibliographies are published by the National Center for Scientific Research (Paris), the *Répertoire* being one of the best annual bibliographies in the field. Divisions include the general history of art, iconography, criticism, libraries and institutes, museums, shows and sales, restoration, topography and archaeology, and monuments with further listings on a chronological and geographical basis. Entries usually carry a brief summary of the contents.

B-14 *Bibliographie zu Kunst und Kunstgeschichte.* Leipzig, 1956—.
Worldwide coverage of bibliography on art theory, iconography, styles, periods, sculpture, painting, architecture, photography, ornament, crafts, and folk art. Indexed.

B-15 Lietzmann, H., ed. *Zeitschrift für Kunstgeschichte, Bibliographie des Jahres . . .* Munich-Berlin.
An annual bibliography of art history almost completely concerned with Western European art. Entries are only listed, not annotated.

B-16 Swoboda, K. M., ed. *Kunstgeschichtische Anzeigen.* Vienna. Published under the auspices of the Art History Institute of the University of Vienna once or twice yearly. Each issue is devoted to different areas of the arts. For example, vol. *6*, nos. 1–2 (1963–64), is concerned with literature on the arts of China and aspects of the Early Middle Ages in publications between 1957 and 1962. Each citation carries a lengthy, useful commentary (in German).

B-17 *Art Index.* New York, 1929—.
A cumulative, pamphlet-sized index to articles in most of the better known art and art history periodicals and many of the

museum bulletins, appearing several times a year. The *Index* is a basic source for early consultation in all research and study. Because it carries book review citations, it is also a partial index of books. All areas of the arts are indexed.

B-18 Lebel, G. *Bibliographie des revues et pēriodiques d'art parus en France de 1746 à 1914* (*Gazette des beaux-arts,* 38, 1951).
A listing of French art magazines for this important period when France was the art center of the world. Annotated as to contents and policy of the citations (in French).

B-19 Rave, P. O. and B. Stein. *Kunstgeschichte in Festschriften.* Berlin, 1962.
One of the "burial places" (because so difficult to know about) for sometimes extremely valuable articles on art is the *Festschrift*—the memorial or commemorative book published in honor of an important teacher or scholar by his friends and disciples. This very helpful bibliography of articles published in *Festschriften* covers the field up to 1960. Alphabetical listing of person honored, listings of articles by contributors, categories, and book titles.

B-20 *Bibliography of the Netherlands Institute for Art History.* The Hague, 1943—.
Brings up-to-date the following item (B-21) with most annotations in English.

B-21 van Hall, H., ed. *Repertorium voor de Geschiedenis der Nederlandsche Schilder—en Graveerkunst.* The Hague, 1936–49.
A two-volume bibliography of Dutch art from the twelfth century on. Typical of the kind of national bibliography produced by many countries, its contents are arranged by subject with author index. Material covered is in all languages; not annotated (See B-20 for continuation.)

B-22 *Schrifttum zur deutschen Kunst.* Berlin, 1958—.
Annual bibliography of German art arranged by types—architecture, painting, sculpture—and indexed by artist, place, and author.

B-23 *Annual Bibliography of the History of British Art.* Cambridge, 1934—.
A typical national bibliography of art with listings arranged by media and special areas, including architecture, painting, sculpture, museums, exhibitions, and iconography. Excludes Roman Britain but includes Celtic and Viking, with brief annotations for items and index.

B-24 Rowland, B., Jr. *Outline and Bibliographies of Oriental Art.* Cambridge, 1945.
A very selective bibliography of only the most critical works on the arts of India, Southeast Asia, Iran, Central Asia, China, and Japan.

B-25 *Subject Index to Literature on Negro Art.* Chicago, 1941.
A bibliography plus index that is now somewhat outdated but still useful.

B-26 Feddersen, M. *Chinese Decorative Art.* London, 1961.
Appended to a general survey of ceramics, metalwork, ivories, lacquer is an extensive bibliography on these subjects.

B-27 Creswell, K. A. C. *A Bibliography of the Architecture, Arts and Crafts of Islam to 1st January 1960.* Cairo, 1961.
The items are arranged by sections on architecture, arts, crafts, and materials (tiles, embroidery, textiles), as well as by country. Index of authors is included.

B-28 Gaskin, L. J. P. *A Bibliography of African Art.* London, 1965.
The volume covers more than 4,500 items and 700 bibliographical references, indexed by author, subject, region, but not annotated.

B-29 Mayer, L. A. and O. Kurz. *Bibliography of Jewish Art.* Jerusalem, 1967.
An account of what has been published about works of Jewish art, 70–1830 A.D. Alphabetical listing by author, brief annotations, and indexed.

B-30 Smith, D. L. *How to Find out in Architecture and Building.* Oxford, 1967.

A "guide to sources of information," it carries sections on careers and training, how to use libraries, bibliographies, periodicals. Primarily designed for the English architectural student, its concern with how to use the library is especially useful.

B-31 Hitchcock, H.-R. *American Architectural Books.* Minneapolis, 1946.
Listed are materials published in the United States prior to 1895, alphabetical by author and annotated in part.

B-32 *Avery Index to Architectural Periodicals.* New York, 1963.
The twelve volumes, plus supplements, carry an index of articles that have appeared in periodicals on architecture, decorative arts, furniture, archaeology, city planning, and housing. There is also a listing by names of architects and subject.

B-33 Levis, H. C. *A Descriptive Bibliography of the Most Important Books in the English Language Relating to the Art and History of Engraving and the Collecting of Prints.* London, 1912.
The article-length title is almost self-explanatory. Included are the catalogs and society and museum publications for engravings and lithography.

B-34 *I.I.C. Abstracts: Abstracts of the Technical Literature on Archaeology and the Fine Arts.* London, 1955—.
A bibliography of items on the materials and techniques of conservation and restoration, as well as information on authentication of objects and forgeries. It contains both author and subject indexes.

B-35 Reisner, R. G. *Fakes and Forgeries in the Fine Arts.* New York, 1950.
A bibliography arranged by area—painting, prints, sculpture—of the period between 1848–1948, with an author index.

B-36 *Katalog der Freiherrlich von Lipperheid'schen Kostümbibliothek.* Berlin, 1896–1905.

This valuable two-volume bibliography on costume with more than 5,000 citations is now available in a facsimile edition (New York, 1963).

B-37 Colas, R. *Bibliographie generale du costume*. Paris, 1969.
A reissue of the 1932–33, two-volume bibliography of more than 3,000 items. Indexed.

B-38 Hiler, H. and M. *Bibliography of Costume*. New York, 1939.
Some 8,400 citations given. This and the previous two works (B-36, B-37) illustrate the type of thorough international coverage that exists in many of the so-called minor arts areas.

B-39 Chandler, A. R. and E. N. Barnhart. *A Bibliography of Psychological and Experimental Aesthetics, 1864–1937*. Berkeley, 1938.
An outdated but valuable general bibliography on psychology and esthetics. Contained in the listings are, for example, studies on color perception, responses to art, art preferences, nature of creativity. Author index. For updated bibliographies on these subjects, see the annual bibliographies published in the *Journal of Aesthetics and Art Criticism* (J-381).

B-40 Kiell, N., ed. *Psychiatry and Psychology in the Visual Arts and Aesthetics: a Bibliography*. Madison, 1965.
Materials on esthetics, art criticism, art therapy, children and art, art of the mentally retarded, psychological analyses and study of artists and their works, psychoses and art, art tests, art ability testing, psychopharmacology and art, etc.

B-41 Hammond, W. A. *A Bibliography of Aesthetics and of the Philosophy of the Fine Arts from 1900–1932*. New York, 1967.
Organized by subject with some annotation and an author index. Its listings can be brought up-to-date by consulting the annual bibliography of esthetics published in the *Journal of Aesthetics and Art Criticism*.

B-42 Clapp, Jane, ed. *Museum Publications*, part 1: *Anthropology, Archaeology, Art*. New York, 1962.

A classified bibliography of publications put out by 276 museums in the United States and Canada: books, pamphlets, monographs, serial reprints, etc. Included are the availability of the items and their prices. Indexed.

ART HISTORY DICTIONARIES

There is a broad array of collections of factual material on the arts that is intended to provide succinct sources of information. They are published under a variety of names: dictionary, handbook, guide, encyclopedia, companion. They cover, in capsule statements, biographies of artists, descriptions of styles and movements, explanations of terms, schools, names, techniques, and periods. Some of these quick reference materials carry only brief citations—a sentence or a paragraph—for each entry, while others, expanded into several volumes, may have some chapter-length discussions on any topic.

Such resource material is not intended to provide the basis for research and study, but rather to give assistance in locating items and meanings, in identifying terms, names, and objects. Usually it provides suggestions for further reading, bibliographies of basic items, that can take the reader into the specialized, in-depth literature on the subject.

Thus, these books should be used, and are most useful for identifying a style or an artist or a technique; for determining the basic, vital statistics of art history; and for defining and describing briefly the geographical and temporal spread of the arts. They should not be used as substitutes for basic source material. It is important to remember that these books aim at covering as much as possible in the least space and do not pretend to go into depth or detail. When used properly—as aids—they are invaluable in saving hours of tedious searching.

Not listed here are the general encyclopedias and dictionaries which are for all areas and are not restricted to art history. However, they should not be forgotten as handy reference tools.

D-44 *Encyclopaedia of World Art.* New York, 1958—.
This McGraw-Hill edition in English of the Italian *Enciclopedia universale dell'arte* is complete in fourteen volumes, plus a classified index volume. The entries are in monograph

form and are not cross-indexed in the several volumes. Hence, it is frequently necessary to go to the index volume first to find the location of the item sought. Each volume is heavily illustrated. The entries are written by some of the most distinguished scholars in the area and carry good, highly selected bibliographies. This encyclopedia is the most ambitious attempt made in English, serving a long-felt need. There is nothing comparable in scope and coverage at the encyclopedia level.

D-45 Myers, B. S., ed. *McGraw-Hill Dictionary of Art.* New York, 1969.
A five-volume dictionary which offers extensive coverage in more than 15,000 entries. Illustrated articles of varying length on techniques, styles, technical terms, artists, museums. Bibliographies are included.

D-46 Huyghe, R., ed. *The Larousse Encyclopaedia of Prehistoric, Ancient, Byzantine, Medieval, Renaissance, Baroque, Modern Art.* New York, 1962—.
The six volumes, one for each of the periods, carry short, informative monographs by periods, written by established authorities in their respective fields. Well illustrated and indexed, they carry no reading lists.

D-47 *Harper's Encyclopedia of Art* (reprinted as *New Standard Encyclopedia of Art.* 1939). New York, 1937.
Contains short articles with bibliographies in two volumes, based on the French edition of about 1925.

D-48 Myers, B. S., ed. *Encyclopedia of Painting.* New York, 1955.
A one-volume, short-entry listing of painters and paintings. Illustrated; useful for very quick, general reference only.

D-49 Cottrell, L., ed. *Concise Encyclopedia of Archaeology.* London, 1960.
World coverage of sites, periods, cultures, movements, techniques, tools, materials, that are met with in the study of

ancient art. A handy one-volume work with a brief bibliography.

D-50 Osborne, H., ed. *The Oxford Companion to Art.* Oxford, 1970.
A very welcome large, single-volume reference for general information. Short-entry form on artists, schools, movements, styles, techniques, with reading lists after each entry. Illustrated and comprehensive, considering the limited space of one volume.

D-51 *Praeger Picture Encyclopedia of Art.* New York, 1958.
A brief, one-volume, heavily illustrated work arranged in chronological order and indexed.

D-52 Runes, D. D. and H. G. Schrickel, eds. *Encyclopedia of the Arts.* New York, 1946.
More than 150 contributors offer a quick reference of uneven quality. No illustrations, but some bibliographical references.

D-53 Schaffran, E. *Dictionary of European Art.* New York, n.d.
Small format, single-volume containing brief entries that are highly selective and uneven with important omissions.

D-54 Murray, P. and L. *Dictionary of Art and Artists.* New York, 1965.
While handy as a quick reference for artists and movements, its chief use is for definitions and explanations of terms, processes, techniques, materials. This lists ample bibliographical material and includes a large selection of photographs.

D-55 Gaunt, W. *Everyman's Dictionary of Pictorial Art.* London, 1962.
Two volumes on painters, periods, art forms, and techniques, with illustrations.

D-56 Wolf, M. L. *Dictionary of the Arts.* New York, 1951.
Definitions and glossary of art terms; no illustrations or bibliography.

D-57 Adeline, J. *Adeline's Art Dictionary.* New York, 1960.
Terms used in the arts and architecture as well as in heraldry, iconography, symbols, and the saints and gods. Small, illustrative drawings. A good dictionary brought up-to-date from the nineteenth-century edition.

D-58 Mayer, R. *A Dictionary of Art Terms and Techniques.* New York, 1969.
Coverage of the terms met most frequently in reading art literature and descriptions of techniques. Illustrated, with a short bibliography.

D-59 Réau, L. *Dictionnaire illustré d'art et d'archéologie.* Paris, 1930.
Dictionary of terms found in art and architecture, short-entry format; in French, but highly recommended for its excellent coverage.

D-60 Réau, L. *L'Art russe, des origines à nos jours.* Paris, 1921–22.
Although this is a short, two-volume history of Russian art, it is included here because of its supplements, which are dictionaries of Russian art terms (vol. *1:* pp. 374–87; vol. *2*; pp. 281–86).

D-61 Mollett, J. W., ed. *An Illustrated Dictionary of Art and Archaeology.* New York, 1966.
Covers a broad range of subjects in the arts, as well as the terms used in the Oriental fields, etymological derivations, festivals, etc. Well illustrated and cross-referenced.

D-62 Réau, L. *Dictionnaire polyglotte des terms d'art et d'archéologie.* Paris, 1953.
A very useful dictionary of terms used in the arts, giving the equivalents in French, Italian, German, English, Spanish, Dutch, Russian, Greek, etc. The primary listing is in French. It also contains a bibliography of dictionaries, lexicons, and glossaries.

D-63 Parow, R. and H. E. Pappenheim. *Kunststile, Kunstsprache.* Munich, 1957.

This contains in the first section a lexicon of styles, schools, movements, and art forms. The second half is an alphabetical listing of terms used in art in German with their French and English equivalents, and the reverse listings (for instance, English terms with their German and French equivalents). Very helpful for translating highly specialized terms in the field (in German).

D-64 Bolotowsky, I. *Russian-English Dictionary of Painting and Sculpture.* New York, 1962.
English-Russian and Russian-English listing of terms and names frequently encountered.

D-65 Kaltenbach, G. E. *Dictionary of Pronunciation of Artists' Names, with their Schools and Dates for American Readers and Students.* Chicago, 1938.
More than 1,500 entries.

D-66 O'Dwyer, J., and R. LeMage. *A Glossary of Art Terms.* New York, 1950.
Very brief entries on terms, techniques, art forms, materials, movements. Useful for specific terms but not for styles, schools.

D-67 Medley, M. *A Handbook of Chinese Art.* London, 1964.
Dictionary of terms in Chinese art literature. A handy, quick-answer reference with many drawings, a select bibliography, and an index.

D-68 Haggar, R. G. *Dictionary of Art Terms.* New York, 1962.
In addition to the dictionary, it includes a glossary of foreign terms and a short bibliography.

D-69 Hansford, S. H. *A Glossary of Chinese Art and Archaeology.* London, 1961.
A small dictionary on bronzes, paintings, ceramics, giving the Chinese characters and transcriptions with English meanings.

D-70 Ware, Dora and Betty Beatty. *A Short Dictionary of Architecture, including some Common Building Terms.* London, 1953.

A dictionary of terms with very brief explanations, illustrated with line drawings, and a bibliography. Good for quick reference.

D-71 Sturgis, R., ed. *A Dictionary of Architecture and Building: Biographical, Historical, and Descriptive.* New York, 1901–1902.
In addition to the terms used in architecture, it provides information on famous buildings, national schools, architectural styles, architects, etc. Illustrated and in two volumes.

D-72 Saylor, H. H. *Dictionary of Architecture.* New York, 1952.
A convenient, pocket-sized dictionary of terms.

D-73 Harris, John and Jill Lever. *Illustrated Glossary of Architecture, 850–1830.* London, 1966.
Short-entry definitions of architectural terms, but see D-74 for fuller definitions. Excellent descriptive photographs and good bibliography.

D-74 Fleming, J., H. Honour, and N. Pevsner. *The Penguin Dictionary of Architecture.* Harmondsworth, 1966.
Very useful, short-entry dictionary with clear illustrative drawings, which gives architectural terms, noted architects, and definitions of building parts.

D-75 Fletcher, Sir Banister. *A History of Architecture on the Comparative Method.* London, 1959.
Reissued (this is the sixteenth edition), it still is the most convenient single-volume reference book for locating quickly data on important architectural monuments. In practical terms, it is a dictionary of buildings, providing worldwide coverage (uneven, it is true, and excluding the last several decades) with identifying photographs, plans, sections, technical information, and history on each building that can be easily located through an excellent index.

D-76 Ramsey, L. G. G., ed. *The Concise Encyclopedia of Antiques.* New York, 1954–61.
Written by several hands and in five volumes, the material is

organized in sections by types of antiques. Indexed by names and places, with bibliography.

D-77 Comstock, H., ed. *The Concise Encyclopedia of American Antiques.* New York, 1965.
A single-volume national encyclopedia, illustrated, and organized alphabetically by subject (for instance, pewter, silver, clocks, rare books, coins and medals, printed maps). Reading lists follow each section. Indexed.

D-78 Drepperd, C. W. *A Dictionary of American Antiques.* Boston, 1952.
Short-entry dictionary of terms found in working with antiques, and also names of craftsmen, artists, companies, and artisans.

D-79 Cowie, D. and K. Henshaw. *Antique Collectors' Dictionary.* New York, 1962.
This covers terms, craftsmen, and objects associated with the field.

D-80 Bernasconi, J. R. *The Collectors' Glossary of Antiques and Fine Arts.* London, 1959.
A dictionary of terms and objects, but it also contains a glossary of saints and their symbols, making it a handy reference.

D-81 Gloag, J. *A Short Dictionary of Furniture.* London, 1966.
A paperback of more than 1,700 terms, illustrated with drawings.

D-82 Aronson, J. *The Encyclopedia of Furniture.* New York, 1965.
Useful book with glossary of designers and craftsmen. Heavily illustrated with photographs and drawings. Bibliography arranged by country.

D-83 Fox-Davies, A. *The Art of Heraldry: an Encyclopaedia of Armory.* New York, 1969.
A history and dictionary of heraldic devices and terms, and a

handbook of motifs and symbols with more than 1,100 drawings.

D-84 Valentine, L. N. *Ornament in Medieval Manuscripts: A Glossary.* London, 1965.
The various ornaments in Western Medieval manuscripts are described, illustrated, and indexed.

ART HISTORY LIBRARY CATALOGS

Several reference and research libraries that specialize in art history holdings have published catalogs of their collections. These catalogs are indispensable, not only for help in locating where published materials are available, but also for working up bibliographies, for finding what printed literature exists on any particular art subject, artist, monument, and topic.

Listed here are several of the most important catalogs available outside of their own libraries. The list is not complete but rather includes the basic published catalogs to provide an idea of the value of these reference tools and a select choice of catalogs for beginning research work.

As mentioned elsewhere, catalogs published by some of the major world libraries, like the British Museum and Library of Congress, should be utilized along with the specialized catalogs.

L-85 *Library Catalog, Metropolitan Museum of Art.* New York.
The basic twenty-five volumes of the catalog are supplemented about every two years with a new volume. The first twenty-three volumes comprise an alphabetical listing of some 147,000 items (in 1960), as well as listings of some periodical articles. The twenty-fourth and twenty-fifth volumes list selected sales catalogs.

L-86 *Index to Art Periodicals, Ryerson Library, Art Institute of Chicago.* Chicago.
The basic eleven volumes and supplements contain citations for articles and illustrations in more than 350 magazines and journals. The material is indexed by subject and artist.

L-87 *Dictionary Catalog of the Library of the Freer Gallery of Art.* Washington, D.C.
Composed of six volumes (1968), it specializes in arts of the Far East, India, Near East, and the painter Whistler. The citations also have summary analyses of the periodical articles listed. Arrangement is by author, subject, and title.

L-88 *Katalog des Kunsthistorischen Instituts in Florenz.* Florence.
In nine volumes plus supplements, the catalog of the Institute for the History of Art specializes in Italian art. The alphabetical index is primarily by author.

L-89 *Library Catalog, Warburg Institute.* London.
The catalog of this art history training center, which is part of the University of London, is based on the personal library of Aby Warburg. Published in ten volumes, the catalog is particularly valuable for bibliography on iconography and symbolism of the arts.

BIOGRAPHICAL DICTIONARIES

It is a simple matter to locate the basic biographical facts on and bibliographical references to the major artists of the past and present in general art history books or by looking them up in the library card catalog. Minor figures in the arts, those about whom books and articles have never been written and who are rarely mentioned other than in local publications, but who were minor lights in local art circles for a short time, can usually be located in biographical dictionaries of the art world.

Listed here are the biographical dictionaries that are most frequently consulted in several fields of the arts. Probably the first place to turn for identifying an artist's name is the "Thieme-Becker" (A-90). Most of the nations of the world have published biographical dictionaries of their artists; only a sampling of these is provided, except for the United States, for which broad coverage is given. The Chamberlin reference (B-1) should be consulted for direction to the dictionaries of any particular country.

A-90 Thieme, U. and F. Becker. *Allgemeines Lexikon der bildenden Künstler, von der Antike bis zur Gegenwart.* Leipzig, 1907–1950.
The standard, most comprehensive listing of artists ever compiled, in thirty-seven volumes. Despite the fact that it is in German, it is the first place to look when trying to identify an artist if one has any knowledge of the language. Each item carries a short biographical sketch, a selected listing of the artist's more important works, and a short reading list.

A-91 Vollmer, H. *Allgemeines Lexicon der bildenden Künstler des XX. Jahrhunderts.* Leipzig, 1953–.
This is a supplement to the "Thieme-Becker" for the twentieth century, with further volumes to come.

A-92 Bénézit, E. *Dictionnaire critique et documentaire des peintres, sculpteurs, dessinateurs et graveurs.* Paris, 1948–1955.
The standard French dictionary in eight volumes. The entries are brief, carrying a few illustrations, noting where works of the artists are to be found, some of the sales prices, and the dates of the sales. There are no bibliographies, but it does carry useful reproductions of the artists' signatures (in French).

A-93 Bryan, M. *Bryan's Dictionary of Painters and Engravers.* London, 1903–1905.
The five-volume reference is outdated but still useful to locate artists. Some artists' monograms are reproduced, and some lists of principal works are given. No bibliographical citations.

A-94 Murray, P. and L. *Dictionary of Art and Artists.* New York, 1965.
Scanty citations useful for quick reference only.

A-95 Mallett, D. T. *Mallett's Index of Artists.* New York, 1948.
An international biographical dictionary with very short entries. It is helpful for lesser known artists, but the information frequently needs to be double-checked for accuracy.

A-96 *Kindlers Malerei Lexikon*. Zurich, 1964—.
The planned six volumes present an alphabetical biography of artists of all times. It gives signatures, with good illustrations in color and black-and-white, selected lists of works of the painters, and bibliography for each entry.

A-97 Fernau, J. *The Praeger Encyclopedia of Old Masters*. New York, 1959.
Useful for quick reference and identification of famous names only.

A-98 Clement, C. E. and L. Hutton. *Artists of the Nineteenth Century and Their Works*. Boston, 1889.
This gives 2,050 biographical sketches in a typical nineteenth-century chatty, anecdotal style. Whereas major figures in nineteenth-century art are frequently omitted—such as Renoir and Monet, for example—lesser lights are given ample treatment. The criticism of art works is hopelessly outdated.

A-99 Édouard-Joseph, R. *Dictionnaire biographique des artistes contemporains*. Paris, 1930–1936.
Three volumes plus supplement of brief biographies of artists who exhibited in France between 1910 and 1930, with a few of the earlier artists included. Its chief value now is for the minor figures listed. Few bibliographical citations; some sales prices, facsimile signatures, photographs of artists, and lists of some of their principal works.

A-100 Maillard, R. and C. Lake, eds. *Dictionary of Modern Painting*. New York, 1964.
Useful for quick identification of an artist or a name from the Impressionists to World War II. It includes some small illustrations and no bibliographies. The list of 250 entries indicates only scattered coverage for the several decades.

A-101 Seuphor, M. (pseudonym of F. L. Berckelaers). *Dictionary of Abstract Painters*. New York, 1957.
Composed in two parts: part 1, a brief history of abstract art; part 2, short notices on artists with bibliography and small identification illustrations.

A-102 Maillard, R., ed. *Dictionary of Modern Sculpture.* New York, 1960.
Brief biographical entries and critiques of the artists and their works. Illustrated, no bibliography.

A-103 Gunnis, R. *Dictionary of British Sculptors, 1660–1851.* London, 1953.
The short biographical entries include some bibliography, lists of major works, places where sculpture is located, and titles.

A-104 Grant, M. H. *A Dictionary of British Sculptors.* London, 1953.
Brief biographical entries with lists of some works and their present locations, as well as indices of sitters and titles of works, but no bibliographies.

A-105 *Avery Obituary Index of Architects and Artists.* Boston, 1963.
An alphabetical listing of deceased architects, some artists, art historians, and city planners that gives bibliographical entries of their obituaries.

A-106 Withey, H. F. and E. R. *Biographical Dictionary of American Architects (Deceased).* Los Angeles, 1956.
Almost 2,000 entries covering the period of about 1740 to 1952. Names of major works are included, but no illustrations.

A-107 Koyl, G. S., ed. *American Architects Directory.* New York, 1962.
A directory rather than biography of American architects, giving professional data on each entry.

A-108 Colvin, H. M. *A Biographical Dictionary of English Architects, 1660–1840.* London, 1954.
Short entries with bibliographies with each citation and indices of persons and places; not illustrated.

A-109 Dutuit, E. *Manuel de l'amateur d'estampes.* Paris, 1881–1888.
The four volumes of this standard work have been reprinted

(1967), providing an index of graphic artists from the various European schools: Italian, German, Flemish, Netherlandish, and English, with illustrations.

A-110 Stauffer, D. M. *American Engravers upon Copper and Steel.* New York, 1907, 1917.
Three-volume (now available in reprint, 1964) illustrated biographical dictionary with checklists of engravings.

A-111 Grant, M. H. *A Dictionary of British Etchers (15th C. to 20th C.).* London, 1952–1953.
Brief biographies with mention of some of the artists' works plus an evaluation. No index or bibliography.

A-112 Hollstein, F. W. H. *German Engravings, Etchings, and Woodcuts, ca. 1400–1700.* Amsterdam, 1951—.
Planned to be complete in twenty to twenty-four volumes, the work will be a comprehensive listing of graphic artists, including small reproductions of their work.

A-113 Andresen, Andreas. *Der deutsche Peintre-Graveur.* Leipzig, 1967.
A five-volume reprint (original edition, 1864–1878) of German artists from the last quarter of the sixteenth century to the end of the eighteenth century with lists of works and facsimile monograms.

A-114 Amstutz, W. *Who's Who in Graphic Art.* Zurich, 1962.
Index of modern designers, illustrators, typographers, cartoonists, but not noncommercial artists. Entries are arranged by country with a photograph of each artist and an illustration of his work.

A-115 Carrick, A. V. L. *A History of American Silhouettes: A Collector's Guide, 1790–1840.* Rutland, 1969.
Some forty artists are listed in this specialized area; illustrated with bibliography and index.

A-116 Bradley, J. W. *A Dictionary of Miniaturists, Illuminators, Calligraphers, and Copyists, with References to their Works, and Notices of their Patrons.* New York, 1958.
A three-volume reprint (original edition 1887–1889) of

alphabetical short citations giving biographies and bibliographical references. Not illustrated.

A-117 Foster, J. A. *A Dictionary of Painters of Miniatures, (1525–1850).* New York, 1967.
Short-entry form without bibliography or illustrations, but the citations do give exhibitions, collections, and sales.

A-118 Darmon, J.-E. *Dictionnaire des peintres miniaturistes sur vêlin, parchemin, ivoire et écaille.* Paris, n.d.
An alphabetical listing of artists on vellum, parchment, ivory, and shell, giving short biographical notices with lists of principal works and some illustrations (in French).

A-119 D'Ancona, P. and E. Aeschlimann. *Dictionnaire des miniaturistes du moyen âge et de la Renaissance.* Milan, 1949.
Short biographical entries by artist with cross-indexing by period, region, and school; illustrated, with bibliographies.

A-120 Forrer, L. *Biographical Dictionary of Medalists, Coin, Gem, and Seal-Engravers, Mint-Masters* (500 B.C.–1900 A.D.). London, 1902–1927.
In seven volumes plus supplements, the dictionary gives identifying marks on works, evaluations, descriptions of coins.

A-121 Pavière, S. H. *A Dictionary of Flower, Fruit, and Still Life Painters.* Leigh-on-Sea, 1962–1964.
Short entry listings covering artists from the fifteenth century through 1885 in three volumes. The dictionary includes not just artists devoted to still life painting, but artists of all genres who painted still lifes. It gives collections, exhibitions, bibliography, and illustrations.

A-122 Grant, M. H. *A Chronological History of the Old English Landscape Painters.* Leigh-on-Sea, 1957.
Chatty commentary and criticism rather than straightforward biography of more than 800 painters in this eight-volume revised edition. Completely indexed in the last volume.

A-123 Young, W., ed. *Dictionary of American Artists, Sculptors, Engravers*. Cambridge, 1968.
Very brief, vital statistics entries on some 18,000 individuals from the beginning to the turn of the twentieth century.

A-124 Groce, G. C. and D. H. Wallace. *The New York Historical Society's Dictionary of Artists in America, 1564–1860*. New Haven, 1964.
More than 10,000 entries giving biography and a couple of reference sources for each artist. There are no listings of works or illustrations, but the dictionary is very useful for first-aid identification of artists in the traditional sense as well as artists in the so-called minor arts, such as cameo cutters, seal cutters, medalists, draftsmen.

A-125 Fielding, M. *Dictionary of American Painters, Sculptors, and Engravers*. New York, 1964.
Very brief entries with a bibliographical reference list at the end of the book.

A-126 *Who's Who in American Art*. New York, 1936—.
Ongoing publication of biographical directory of artists, art historians, museum personnel, critics, editors, and others affiliated with the arts.

A-127 Smith, R. C. *A Biographical Index of American Artists*. Baltimore, 1930.
Some 4,700 short-entry listings with references to biographical source materials.

A-128 Michigan State Library. *Biographical Sketches of American Artists*. Lansing, 1924.
A very selected list of painters, sculptors, illustrators, glass designers, and etchers. Useful only for finding some lesser known figures that may not appear in other dictionaries.

A-129 Cummings, P. *A Dictionary of Contemporary American Artists*. New York, 1966.
Short-entry listings giving professional careers of the artists only. Illustrated and with a general bibliography.

A-130 Redgrave, S. *A Dictionary of Artists of the English School.* London, 1878.
Once again available (reprinted 1967), this directory lists painters, sculptors, architects, engravers, and ornamentists with short biographies, listings of major works, and some "evaluation" of quality.

A-131 Cunningham, A. *The Lives of the Most Eminent British Painters, Sculptors, and Architects.* London, 1830–1833.
Six volumes of fairly long essays arranged alphabetically.

A-132 *Who's Who in Art.* London, 1927—.
Continuing publication of biographies of leading British artists, with facsimile signatures and monograms.

A-133 Graves, A. *The Royal Academy of Arts: a Complete Dictionary of Contributors and their Work from its Foundation in 1769 to 1904.* London, 1905–1906.
An alphabetical listing in eight volumes of artists with a year by year list of titles of works exhibited for each.

A-134 Contag, V. and Chi-Ch'ien Wang. *Seals of Chinese Painters and Collectors of the Ming and Ch'ing Periods.* Hong Kong, 1966.
Facsimile reproductions of the seals with Chinese and German annotations, in two volumes.

A-135 Waley, A. *An Index of Chinese Artists.* London, 1922.
Alphabetically arranged by family name, then personal name, and cross-listed by pseudonyms; English and Chinese characters.

A-136 Society of Friends of Eastern Art. *Index of Japanese Painters.* Tokyo, 1958.
Approximately 600 short biographies and listing of Japanese schools; English entries with names also in Japanese characters.

A-137 Strickland, W. G. *Dictionary of Irish Artists.* Dublin, 1913.
The two-volume edition gives drawings and photographs of artists, along with lists of major works, but no references.

A-138 Wurzbach, A. *Niederländisches Künstler Lexikon.* Vienna, 1906–1911.
Biographical dictionary in three volumes of Dutch and Flemish artists up to the nineteenth century.

A-139 Brun, C. *Schweizerisches Künstler-Lexikon.* Frauenfeld, 1905–1917.
Recently reprinted (1967), the three-volume dictionary carries short entries on Swiss artists, with selected bibliographies.

A-140 Immerzeel, J. *De Levens en Werken der hollandsche en vlaamche Kunstschilders, Beeldhouwers, Graveurs en Bouwmeesters.* Amsterdam, 1855.
Lives of Dutch and Flemish artists from the 15th century to 1840 in three volumes.

National Biographical Dictionaries. There are, in addition to specialized dictionaries such as those listed above, general, national biographical dictionaries. These multi-volume works can be used as references additional to the art history biographical dictionaries, not as substitutes. They are most helpful in the identification of sitters for portrait paintings and sculpture, as well as for patrons of artists, collectors, friends of artists, etc. Probably all lands have one or more national dictionaries of biography; listed here is only a sample from English-speaking lands.

A-141 *Dictionary of American Biography.* New York, 1928–1958.

A-142 Wallace, W. S. *The Macmillan Dictionary of Canadian Biography.* London, 1963.
Canadians who died before 1961.

A-143 *Dictionary of Canadian Biography.* Toronto, 1966—.

A-144 *Dictionary of National Biography.* London, 1908.
Standard for British biography.

ART AND ART HISTORY REFERENCE AIDS

Gathered here is a broad variety of general reference aids useful in the study, handling, collecting, and teaching of the several arts.

Museum Guides and Directories. No doubt the tremendous growth in tourism in the past two decades is at least partly responsible for a steady increase in the number of guidebooks to the major museums and monuments of America and Western Europe. These books are valuable not only as guides for the visitor but also for the locating and documenting of works and the discovering of what collections exist and what they hold.

Several commercial publishers issue travel guides to countries and cities (such as Nagel's guides, Michelin guidebooks, and Baedeker handbooks) which, in addition to giving general tourist information, detail local museums, monuments, and famous buildings. Many of the large cities, particularly in Europe, sponsor guidebooks with itineraries and listings of their art and monumental treasures—for example, London has been updating for several decades its *Guide to London Museums and Galleries* (H. M. Stationery Office, 1953, 5th ed.), and New York has a *Greater New York Art Directory* (ed. T. J. Scott, Center for Urban Education, 1968)—have inexpensive directories to their collections and art establishments.

Almost all major museums and many small ones issue pamphlet-sized guides to their collections, while most great collections have detailed published catalogs of all or part of their holdings, lavishly illustrated. These catalogs are important source books for study of individual works of art, and the smaller guidebooks are excellent companions on tours of museums.

It is not desirable or practical to list all or even a broad sampling of the guides and catalogs that have been published. The few provided below are those which are most useful to the American student and traveler. Included are a few citations of different kinds of guides sufficient to indicate the variety of materials now easily available.

R-145 *Museums Directory of the United States and Canada.* Washington, 1965.

This is the second edition of a comprehensive listing of more than 5,000 institutions, organized by type of museum. Each citation gives the address of the museum, names of curatorial staff, types of collections, major activities of the museum, and the governing authority. An excellent directory for North American collections.

R-146 Katz, Herbert and Marjorie. *Museums, U.S.A.: A History and Guide*. New York, 1965.
A popular history of American museums, founders of museums, and major collectors in the United States. The appendix lists the museums by state and city, with a brief indication of the contents of their collections. R-145 is preferable for a full listing of American museums.

R-147 Cartwright, W. A. *Guide to Art Museums in the United States*. New York, 1958—.
A projected series of guides to American collections. The first one, for example, covers twenty-five galleries on the East Coast, from Washington to Miami.

R-148 Spaeth, E. *American Art Museums and Galleries*. New York, 1960.
A small book for visitors to museums with a selected list arranged by geographical area. It is indexed and provides names of museum people, price ranges of various art works, and other incidental information.

R-149 *A Guide to Asian Collections in American Museums*. New York, 1964.
A pamphlet published by Asia House (New York) giving a brief description of oriental collections in forty-four museums. It provides a general summary of the nature of the museum's holdings, the size of the collection, items of special interest, addresses, and hours available to the public.

R-150 Faison, S. L. *Art Museums of New England*. New York, 1958.
A directory of museums and collections, listed alphabetically by state, plus a selected listing of historic buildings. The index contains names of the important artists represented in the collections.

R-151 Braider, D. *Putnam's Guide to the Art Centers of Europe.* New York, 1965.
A brief guide, arranged by country and city, to the major museums, collections, monuments, and buildings of Europe. Each reference includes a description of the museum or monument, its history, and the objects of major importance. Helpful index of artists, architects, and locations of artists' works. A very handy travel guide.

R-152 Stadler, W. *European Art: a Traveller's Guide.* Edinburgh, 1960.
A translation of the German *Führer,* it lists more than 800 European collections.

R-153 *Itinerari dei musei e monumenti d'Italia.* Rome, variously dated.
A multi-volume series of guide pamphlets to individual museums of Italy. The notations are brief, as appropriate for a pocket museum guide, with small identification illustrations.

R-154 *Museums and Galleries in Great Britain and Ireland.* London, 1965–1966.
A guide providing in alphabetical order by city the collections of the British Isles. Included is a cross-listing by museums and a subject index.

R-155 *World of Art Library: Galleries.*
A series of heavily illustrated volumes on some of the greatest art collections of the world produced by the London publishing house, Thames and Hudson. An excellent source for major works with a checklist of such works and succinct commentaries on major pieces. Included in the series are:

Bazin, G. *The Louvre.* 1966.

Bazin, G. *The Impressionist Paintings in the Louvre,* 1961.

Canton, F. J. S. *The Prado.* 1966.

Descargues, P. *The Hermitage.* 1961.

Dorival, B. *The School of Paris: Musée de l'art moderne,* 1962.

Hendy, P. *The National Gallery, London,* 1963.

Mentz, H. *The Dresden Gallery.* 1962.

Rossi, P. *The Uffizi and Pitti.* 1967.

Rothenstein, J. *The Tate Gallery.* 1962.

Van Luttervelt, R. *Dutch Museums.* 1960.

Walker, J. *The National Gallery, Washington.* 1964.

R-156 Tietze, H. *Treasures of the Great National Galleries.* London, 1955.

A well illustrated introduction to the Vienna Picture Gallery, Uffizi (Florence), Louvre (Paris), Prado (Madrid), Rijksmuseum (Amsterdam), Berlin Picture Gallery, National Gallery (London), National Gallery of Art (Washington), Budapest Museum of Fine Arts, Brussels Museum of Fine Arts, Munich Picture Gallery, Dresden Picture Gallery, Brera (Milan), Academy (Venice), Vatican Picture Gallery, Metropolitan Museum of Art (New York).

R-157 Cooper, Douglas, ed. *Great Private Collections.* London, 1963.

An illustrated account of twenty-six great private collections of art. Unfortunately, it is not indexed and, therefore, there is no way of quickly locating which collection houses a specific work if one only has the name of the artist or object.

Directories of People in the Arts (other Than Artists)

R-158 *International Directory of Arts.* Berlin, 1965–1966.

This is the eighth revised, two-volume edition of a worldwide listing of people and institutions affiliated with the arts. Volume *1* contains names and addresses of museums, art galleries, schools, colleges, artists, collectors, art associations. Volume *2* contains names and addresses of art and antique dealers, galleries, art publishers, art periodicals, art booksellers, restorers, experts, dealers.

R-159 Gilbert, D. B., ed. *American Art Directory.* New York.
An annual listing of art museums, universities, college art departments, art schools, museums, and schools in America as well as some in Europe.

R-160 *Mastai's Classified Directory of American Art and Antique Dealers.* New York, 1961.
This is the seventh edition of the listing of art museums, dealers, etc. It also contains lists of museums in Canada, Mexico, Belgium, the British Isles, France, Switzerland, and the Netherlands. It includes some information on dealers in color prints and prices for art works sold at auction.

Buying and Selling Works of Art. One of the most often asked, and most difficult of questions to answer, is the money value of a work of art. Art prices fluctuate constantly and often dramatically. One aid in assessing financial value is an examination of the price that works by particular artists have brought in the past. The references listed here provide such information, which is useful not only for the person interested in the finances of art, but also for the art historian who traces the history of a work of art as it moved from artist to collectors.

Because art prices are highly speculative, manipulated, subject to fads, fancies, and whims, dependent on rarity and availability of objects, and because they react to fashions and general market trends, there is no book which tells what any work of art is worth; all that can be told is what prices works fetched in the past. Whenever one is dealing with prices paid in the past, he must remember that these prices are relative, not absolute. The prices are meaningful only if they are considered within the context of the value of money at that particular time of the sale (thus, for example, $10,000 paid for a work of art during a depression is far more "money" than the same sum paid during a period of inflation).

It is gratuitous to add that there is no necessary relationship between the money evaluation of a work of art and its worth as a work of art.

R-161 Reitlinger, G. *The Economics of Taste.* London, 1961, 1963.

These two volumes chronicle the fluctuating market in the buying and selling of paintings and *objêts d'art* from mid-eighteenth century to 1960. They provide lists by artist of prices paid for individual works. Indexes are arranged by artists, collectors, and dealers. The second volume includes a bibliography.

R-162 Lugt, F. *Rêpertoire des catalogues de ventes publiques intêr-essant l'art ou la curiositê.* The Hague, 1938, 1953, 1964.
The first two volumes list sales catalogs of Europe issued between 1600–1860; the third volume covers the period 1861–1900. Dates and places of sales with an index of collections sold are included. For sales catalogs after 1900, see listings in the published catalog of the Metropolitan Museum of Art (L-85).

R-163 Lancour, A. H. *American Art Auction Catalogues, 1785–1942.* New York, 1944.
Listed are more than 7,000 sales catalogs, with a directory of auction houses and an index of collectors.

R-164 *Art Prices Current.* London, 1907—.
A continuing series publishing the prices paid for art works at principal auctions. It provides names of artists, works of art, and purchasers. Contents are arranged by medium, and each volume is indexed by the name of artist and collector.

R-165 *Art-Price Annual.* London.
An annual publication of auction prices arranged by categories, such as antiques, pictures, manuscripts.

R-166 *World Collectors Annuary.* Delft, 1964—.
A continuing listing of works of art sold in Europe and America, arranged alphabetically by artist. Volume nineteen, for example, lists more than 6,200 items sold at auction in 1967.

R-167 *Print Prices Current.* London, 1918—.
A continuing series of auction sales of engravings, etchings, and Baxter prints in Great Britain and America. It is indexed by artist.

Art Catalogs. One of the most useful tools in art research is the annotated catalog of art works compiled usually for an exhibition, for a sale or auction, or for the permanent collections of a museum, gallery, or individual. A well researched catalog gives in short-entry form such facts on each work of art as the medium, authorship, dimensions, date, present and past owners, physical condition, prior exhibitions, and bibliography. Frequently, it also gives iconographic sources for the work, as well as details of when and how it was made, of its place in the *oeuvre* of the artist and of the artist's period and time, and of its broader significance within the historical framework. While the beginning student in art history, concerned with gaining mastery of the broader aspects of the field, infrequently has recourse to catalogs, the advanced student will find them indispensable for locating and documenting works of art.

These catalogs are not exhaustive in that they cover only those works by an artist in that particular collection, sale, and exhibition. But complete catalogs of artists' works (as complete, that is, as any such work can be) of major and minor figures do exist. Thus, to locate or learn the statistical facts on a specific work by a known artist, the first place to look would be in a published catalog of his works, *providing* that one has been compiled.

Most large and many small museums, as well as many famous private collections, have published catalogs of their major holdings. Collections are constantly being augmented; it is not uncommon for a catalog to be somewhat outdated almost before it is in print because of acquisitions made between the time of writing and when the list comes off the presses. Newly found works by artists are constantly being uncovered or finally authenticated; others may be removed because of a reattribution or discovery of a forgery or copy. While such changes are very important, they do not diminish the importance of these catalogs.

Only a few years ago catalogs of exhibitions, sales, and collections provided little more than the statistics of title, dimensions, and owner of each object shown with a pitiful handful of inadequate photographs. However, it is increasingly popular now for catalogs to document fully every entry and to include excellent and abundant illustrations, making the publication a valuable art history reference work that goes beyond the scope of the works listed. Today catalogs are often book-sized, scholarly productions and not just "guides" to an exhibition.

To locate catalogs of works of artists, one should go to the card catalog of the library and look under the artists' names. Catalogs of collectors and museums will be listed under their proper names. Locating catalogs of sales is more difficult, but the several types of catalogs cited offer a great deal of help; a very wide range, of international scope, of exhibition catalogs can be found in the entry below.

R-168 *Worldwide Art Catalogue Bulletin.* New York.
A quarterly published by Worldwide Books which lists art catalogs of current exhibitions around the world that can be purchased (but not exclusively) from this company. Each entry is briefly annotated and gives the price of the catalog and how to order. The *Bulletin* is indexed by medium, period, and subject. Each issue carries about 400 listings.

Reproductions, Photographs, Slides, and Films. Photographs and reproductions of most art objects can be obtained either from the collection that holds the object or from commercial firms specializing in the production and sale of illustrative material. Most museums have a small selection of their holdings reproduced in slide transparencies, but most commercial slides are produced and sold by special companies. Filmstrips and motion pictures are obtained through distributors.

Public museums sell black-and-white photographs of works in their collections. The fee for a glossy print may run from fifty cents to three dollars, plus postage. Requests can be addressed to the museum's registrar or sales desk in the United States, and in care of the director for European collections.

Private museums will usually provide photographs of their holdings, also, but frequently their charges are higher than those of public institutions. If a private museum does not already have a photographic negative for the object in question, it may also charge for the negative (which is not sent to the purchaser), as well as for the print. Thus, it is always well to inquire about costs before ordering a photograph from a private institution.

Private collectors rarely, if ever, have available copies of photographs of their art works. Some collectors have a standing arrangement with a photographer who will supply prints, or their collections may be represented in the files of some of the commercial houses that produce photographs. If a work owned by a private collector has been on exhibition at a museum, that museum may have a negative but probably will not release a print without the owner's permission. Hence, the first step in acquiring a photograph of an art object in a private collection is to contact the owner to ascertain whether or not a photograph is available, the cost of obtaining one, or whether he will grant permission to obtain a copy from a museum that has a negative. Private collectors frequently give objects to museums on a permanent loan basis. The museum probably has a photograph of such pieces, but a request to the museum for a photograph must be accompanied by the written permission of the object's owner.

Art dealers usually have photographs of works in their collections that are for sale. The degree of cooperation in providing photographs to students and scholars varies with the dealer. An art dealer is more interested in selling works of art than photographs of the works.

Several commercial companies provide photographic reproductions of art works; they have a large file of negatives of works from both public and private collections. Usually these companies are best stocked with illustrations of works from or in their own country. Some of the companies have catalogs of their holdings (various ones are listed below), but many do not. The cost of obtaining photographs from a commercial house is not necessarily higher than it would be if one went directly to the owner.

Photographs can be made from printed illustrations in books and periodicals. Best results are obtained by photocopying—taking a photograph of the printed illustration. But even the best photocopy will have its shortcomings, sometimes tending to be gray or lacking in contrast or sharpness of detail, and it repeats all the flaws that may be present in the original photograph and the subsequent printing in the book. Libraries now often have dry copying machines of several kinds that reproduce a page from a book in a couple of minutes for about a dime. These are inferior reproductions, but they are extremely useful for home study purposes as a visual "notating" of the general aspect of a work of art.

With a camera and careful practice, one can take his own photographs and slide transparencies (see R-204, R-203). Museums have different policies on permitting photography in the galleries; time, frustration, and embarrassment can be saved by determining a museum's policy prior to a visit.

Public monuments and buildings are freely photographed, but it is courteous and may be legally necessary to obtain permission before photographing private buildings or works. In Europe, for example, one may expect to find at the entrance to some ancient monuments and churches notices that restrict or forbid the use of cameras. It is always courteous to ask permission of an owner or attendant before photographing inside such a building.

Obtaining permission to photograph an art work, or obtaining a photograph from a museum or collector, does not carry with it the permission to use the photograph for purposes other than private study. Hence, one must always seek permission of the owner of the art object and of the producer of the photograph before using it for other purposes. Copyright laws are equally binding on copying illustrations from books.

A broad range of companies producing or distributing films on art issue pamphlet catalogs of their films for sale and for rent, and the audio-visual divisions of some universities (for example, Iowa, Indiana, Kentucky, Illinois), and public libraries have catalogs of these instructional materials. In addition to the citations given later, listed here are a selected few of the commercial film distributors:

Award Winning Films on Art, Henk Newenhouse Inc., 1017 Longaker Road, Northbrook, Ill.

Contemporary Films, Inc., 267 W. 25th St., New York, N.Y.

International Film Bureau, Inc., 57 E. Jackson Blvd., Chicago, Ill.

McGraw-Hill Films, 330 West 42nd St., New York, N.Y.

Canadian Centre for Films on Art, P.O. Box 457, Ottawa, Ontario, Canada

R-169 UNESCO. *Catalogue of Color Reproductions prior to 1860.* Paris, 1968.

An illustrated catalog of 1,041 paintings, with notations of size, dealer, and price.

R-170 UNESCO. *Catalogue of Colour Reproductions of Paintings 1860 to 1965.* Paris, 1966.
Illustrated catalog of almost 1,600 paintings, listed by painters, publishers, printers, with details on size and purchasing.

R-171 *Alinari catalogo delle fotografie di opere d'arte e vedute.* Florence, 1920–1940.
Alinari is the chief single supplier of high quality photographs of works of art. This catalog, in thirty volumes, also gives addresses of local (United States) outlets for purchasing.

R-172 *Alinari mille pitture di venti secoli: Paintings of Twenty Centuries.* Florence, 1949.
Catalog of color prints available through Alinari.

R-173 Nunn, G. W. A. *British Sources of Photographs and Pictures.* London, 1952.
This lists photographers and their addresses, libraries, museums, art institutions, and journals. It contains a subject index.

R-174 New York Graphic Society. *Fine Art Reproductions of Old and Modern Masters.* Greenwich, 1968.
A listing of color reproductions for sale through this company. It contains color illustrations of all prints available, giving dimensions and prices; arranged chronologically and indexed.

R-175 Faye, Helen. *Picture Sources: An Introductory List.* New York, 1959.
A bibliography of picture sources arranged by company, institution, etc. The listing of companies dealing in "Fine, Graphic, and Applied Arts" is particularly applicable here.

R-176 Clapp, Jane. *Art Reproductions.* New York, 1961.
A list of reproductions for sale in museums in the United States and Canada. Indexed by artist, location, subject.

R-177 Brooke, M., and H. J. Dubester. *Guide to Color Prints.* Washington, 1953.
A listing of some 5,000 color reproductions for sale in the United States, arranged by artist and by title of work.

R-178 Bartran, M. *A Guide to Color Reproductions.* New York, 1966.
A list of 8,500 titles available for purchase. It provides information on publishers of reproductions, prices, dimensions, and names of dealers.

R-179 *University Prints.* Cambridge, Mass.
This company (University Prints, Cambridge, Mass. 02138) makes available a complete catalog of 6,600 black-and-white study prints covering the history of art. The reproductions cost but a few pennies each and can be ordered in loose sheets or bound in any combination desired. Such sets of illustrations can be designed for any course and are excellent study aids in basic classes.

R-180 Myers, B. S. *Art and Civilization: Teacher's Manual.* New York, 1967.
This manual contains a selected list of color print, slide, film, and filmstrip dealers in the United States and abroad.

R-181 *The American Library Compendium and Index of World Art.* New York, 1961.
One of the largest producers of black-and-white and color transparencies for sale, the American Library's transparencies are inexpensive on large orders.

R-182 Monro, I. S. and K. M. *Index to Reproductions of European Paintings: A Guide to Pictures in More than Three Hundred Books.* New York, 1956.
Entries are listed by artist, title, and some subjects.

R-183 Monro, I. S. and K. M. *Index to Reproductions of American Paintings.* New York, 1948.
The companion volume to R-182, but with broader coverage, with more than 800 books.

R-184 Clapp, Jane. *Sculpture Index.* Metuchen, 1970.
A two volume "guide to pictures of sculpture . . . in about 950 publications" organized alphabetically by artist, title, subject, and country.

R-185 Cirker, H. and B., eds. *Dictionary of American Portraits.* New York, 1967.

More than 4,000 illustrations of famous Americans from earliest times to the beginning of the twentieth century in alphabetical order.

R-186 Singer, H. W. *Neuer Bildniskatalog.* Leipzig, 1937–1938.
A five-volume companion volume to R-187, providing an index to painted and sculptured portraits.

R-187 Singer, H. W. *Allgemeiner Bildniskatalog.* Leipzig, 1930–1936.
This fourteen-volume companion to R-186 has now been reprinted (1967). It indexes sources for engraved reproductions of portraits.

R-188 Lane, W. C. and N. E. Browne, eds. *A.L.A. Portrait Index.* Washington, 1906.
An index to portraits contained in printed books and periodicals, this tells where to find more than 120,000 portraits of some 35,000 to 40,000 individuals.

R-189 Masciotta, M. *Portraits d'artistes par eux-mêmes, xive-xxe siècle.* Milan, 1955.
A picture album containing more than 260 self-portraits of artists. Indexed.

R-190 Chapman, W. McK. *Films on Art, 1952.* Kingsport, 1952.
A directory of films and film sources. Alphabetical title and subject index. It also contains material on the use of films on art and their history.

R-191 Humphrys, A. W. *Films on Art.* Washington, 1964.
A listing of films and addresses of producers and distributors with indication of appropriate school grade level and costs.

HANDLING WORKS OF ART

Because of the great value, and often times the extreme fragility of art objects, the physical protection, conservation, and photographing of art objects are important subjects. Also, in the handling of art works, the vexing problems of copies, forgeries, and reproductions are significant. Also, in dealing in works of art, there are complicated, highly specialized legal requirements. The following books cover these various topics.

R-192 Smith, R. C. *A Bibliography of Museums and Museum Work.* Washington, 1928.
A bibliography, now somewhat outdated, on materials about museum work.

R-193 Dudley, D. H. and I. Bezold. *Museum Registration Methods.* Washington, 1958.
A very useful handbook on the practical operations and duties of a museum registrar. Contents include the function of the registration department, techniques of registering, measuring, marking, storing, packing, shipping, accessioning, cataloging, classifying, and caring for art objects. Indexed.

R-194 Plenderleith, H. J. *The Conservation of Antiquities and Works of Art.* London, 1956.
An expert, detailed manual on treatment, repair, restoration, and methods of preservation by one of the top authorities in the field.

R-195 Keck, C. *A Handbook on the Care of Paintings.* Nashville, 1965.
A well illustrated handbook on the conservation of art works. Appended are lists of major American conservators, suppliers of conservation materials, and a good bibliography.

R-196 Stout, G. L. *The Care of Pictures.* New York, 1948.
A very good manual with excellent technical illustrations on construction of pictures, defects, damage, weaknesses, repairing, cleaning, housing, handling, and moving. Indexed, with full bibliography.

R-197 Savage, G. *The Art and Antique Restorer's Handbook.* New York, 1967.
This details the materials and processes of repair and restoration with very useful practical instructions.

R-198 Ruhemann, H. *The Cleaning of Paintings, Problems and Potentialities.* New York, 1968.
A technical handbook with a historical background of the field of restoration, with bibliography and index.

R-199 Kurz, O. *Fakes.* New York, 1967.
A revised edition (earlier edition 1948) giving a good description of the techniques and methods of forgery.

R-200 Schüller, S. *Forgers, Dealers, Experts.* London, 1960.
An anecdotal account of some of the great art forgeries.

R-201 Mendax, F. *Art Fakes and Forgeries.* London, 1955.
A readable history of the subject.

R-202 Savage, G. *Forgeries, Fakes, and Reproductions.* New York, 1963.
Provides technical information on detecting and uncovering forgeries, with appendices on the various techniques, such as ultraviolet radiation and X-ray. Well illustrated with extensive bibliography and index.

R-203 Lewis, J., and E. Smith. *Reproducing Art.* New York, 1969.
Instructions on how to photograph flat and three-dimensional objects in color and black-and-white. The book assumes the reader already understands photography and photographic processing. The authors also carry the discussion through the mechanical processes of book printing from color illustrations.

R-204 Matthews, S. K. *Photography in Archaeology and Art.* London, 1968.
A technical manual for photographing paintings and objects. The first part gives a history of photographic processes; the second part discusses optics, lenses, exposure meters, emulsions, copying, color processes, and photographing. Bibliography.

R-205 Hodes, S. *The Law of Art and Antiquities.* Dobbs Ferry, New York, 1966.
The legal ramifications of buying, selling, renting, commis-

sioning, copyrighting, and contracting for works of art. This also contains information on income tax laws, donations, contributions, and customs tariffs.

R-206 Nagler, G. K. *Die Monogrammisten.* Munich, 1858—.
An early, but still useful five-volume alphabetical listing of monograms and their identification.

R-207 Einstein, M. I. D., and M. A. Goldstein, eds. *Collectors Marks.* St. Louis, 1918.
Useful for identification of collectors by their marks and monograms, arranged in alphabetical order by collector.

THE ARTS AS CRAFTS

There is an almost never-ending array of books, pamphlets, handbooks, guides, and manuals on the techniques, materials, and practices of the several art forms. Such material ranges from the highly professional technical handbook to the amateur's how-to-do-it-in-ten-easy-steps manual. Listed here are one or two of the professional books in each of the major areas. Appended to this list is a helpful volume on job opportunities in the arts and a book of selections from art historical writing in German for the beginning graduate student in art history.

R-208 Constable, W. G. *The Painter's Workshop.* London, 1953.
A discussion of past techniques and materials.

R-209 Mayer, R. *The Artist's Handbook of Materials and Techniques.* New York, 1957.
This is concerned with the various painting techniques.

R-210 Doerner, M. *The Materials of the Artist and Their Use in Painting.* New York, 1962.
One of the basic books in the area of painting.

R-211 Rich, J. C. *The Materials of Sculpture.* New York, 1947.

R-212 Peterdi, G. *Printmaking: Methods Old and New.* New York, 1959.

A very technical handbook for the printmaker which covers all phases except lithography.

R-213 Heller, Jules. *Printmaking Today*. New York, 1958.
This technical material seems to have been designed with the amateur in mind.

R-214 Weaver, Peter. *The Technique of Lithography*. New York, 1964.

R-215 Brunsdon, J. *The Technique of Etching and Engraving*. New York, 1965.

R-216 *The Pictorial Cyclopedia of Photography*. South Brunswick, 1968.

R-217 Morton, Philip. *Contemporary Jewelry: A Studio Handbook*. New York, 1970.
A college-level text.

R-218 Untracht, O. *Metal Techniques for Craftsmen*. New York, 1968.

R-219 Chieffo, C. T. *Silk-Screen as a Fine Art: A Handbook of Contemporary Silk-screen Printing*. New York, 1967.

R-220 Holden, D. *Art Career Guide: A Guidance Handbook for Art Students, Teachers, Vocational Counselors, Parents and Job Hunters*. New York, 1967.
The guide discusses careers in art, choosing an art school, finding a job, preparing credentials and portfolios, exhibiting. It includes a directory of degree-granting schools, professional organizations, and guidance agencies. Particularly useful for the high school art major and art school student.

R-221 Bieber, M. *German Readings*. Philadelphia, 1958.
Designed to help the graduate art history student learn the specialized vocabulary developed at the very beginning of the study of art history by the Germans, it provides selected readings from the "classical" art historians (for example, Riegl, Buschor, Rodenwalt, Goethe, Lessing, Winckelmann), with a vocabulary.

ICONOGRAPHY

Iconography (from the Greek *eikōn*-likeness, image) in its broadest, modern usage concerns the identification of figures, themes, concepts, and motifs depicted in art. It includes information found in the many fields of religion, mythology, folklore, biography, history. The symbols, signs, attributes, tokens, and emblems must be identified and understood when dealing with art works of different periods and cultures. This section contains sources for quick reference to the identification of such subject matter in greater depth than the abbreviated entries in general dictionaries and encyclopedias. These reference works are helpful in answering questions of the following type:

What are the meanings of the different scenes in the life of the Buddha represented in the reliefs at Amaravati?

What are the *mudrās* of the Buddha?

What are the meanings of the mandorla, halo, *nimbus, vesica piscus*?

What does the Greek inscription *Chi-Rho* refer to on a Christian sarcophagus?

How can the figure of a saint holding a broken wheel be identified?

What is the story of Saint Ursula and the Ten Thousand Virgins that appears in Venetian painting?

Who is the Cumean sibyl painted on the Sistine chapel ceiling?

Who were the Greek chthonic gods sometimes represented in Greek vase painting?

What are the avatars of Brahma that are depicted in Hindu art?

The reference works listed here are primarily concerned with religious and mythological (that is, sacred) iconography. Secular iconography—the identification of portraits of people as they appear in works of art—covers the entire range of history.

R-222 Cirlot, J. E. *A Dictionary of Symbols*. London, 1962.
A 400-page, single-volume dictionary.

R-223 *Oxford Classical Dictionary*. Oxford, 1964.
The standard one-volume dictionary for the Classical world,

covering history, mythology, religion, politics, arts, language, and geography.

R-224 Zimmerman, J. E. *Dictionary of Classical Mythology.* New York, 1964.
A short-entry, easy-to-use dictionary giving phonetic pronunciation for each item. It also includes important historical figures.

R-225 Oswalt, S. G. *Concise Encyclopedia of Greek and Roman Mythology.* Glasgow and Chicago, 1969.
A handy, one-volume, pocketbook edition includes charts of the family trees of the gods and heroes.

R-226 Smith, W., ed. *Dictionary of Greek and Roman Biography and Mythology.* London, 1844.
A three-volume old but still very useful dictionary of short citations with an excellent listing of minor figures. It provides references to classical sources in literature.

R-227 Seyffert, O. *Dictionary of Classical Antiquities.* New York, 1956.
A very handy paperback revision of the 1891 edition, covering mythology, religion, literature, and the arts of the Graeco-Roman world.

R-228 Bulfinch, Thomas. *The Age of Fable.* New York, 1966.
This is the paperback edition of the classic retelling of Greek and Roman myths and legends, with an index of names and the geneology of the gods.

R-229 Frazer, J. G. *The New Golden Bough.* Ed. T. H. Gaster. New York, 1959.
A most welcome abridgment, plus additional notes and references, of one of the classics on primitive religious thought, folk customs, and myths (the *golden bough*). This edition is very serviceable because the several volumes of the original writings of Frazer have become difficult to manage, except for the specialist in the area.

R-230 Edwardes, M. and L. Spence. *A Dictionary of Non-Classical Mythology.* London, 1937.

A reprint of one of the Everyman's Library reference book series. A good general, short-entry reference for *all* myths, but see R-231 below.

R-231 Sykes, E. *Everyman's Dictionary of Non-Classical Mythology*. London, 1952.
Preferable to previous edition (see R-230 above) because of increased number of entries.

R-232 Künstle, K. *Ikonographie der christlichen Kunst*. Freiburg *im Breisgau*, 1926–1928.
A two-volume alphabetical listing of saints and holy figures, Christian motifs. An excellent source book, but in German; indexed, with bibliographies.

R-233 Aurenhammer, H. *Lexikon der christlichen Ikonographie*. Vienna, 1959—.
This lexicon of Christian iconography, in the process of being published in sections, is arranged in alphabetical order, with extensive coverage and bibliographies.

R-234 Woodruff, H. *The Index of Christian Art at Princeton University: A Handbook*. Princeton, 1942.
This handbook describes the index of early Christian and medieval iconography maintained at Princeton. Available to graduate students, as well as advanced scholars, it is the largest single collection of its kind.

R-235 Réau, L. *Iconographie de l'art chrêtien*. Paris, 1955–1959.
Published in six parts as three volumes, this French reference work covers the iconography of Old and New Testament figures, their attributes, symbols, and representations, with bibliographical citations.

R-236 Goldsmith, E. E. *Sacred Symbols in Art*. New York, 1912.
A dictionary of Christian attributes, symbols, and saints.

R-237 Ferguson, G. W. *Signs and Symbols in Christian Art*. New York, 1954.
A dictionary of saints, holy figures, symbols, signs, religious objects, emblems, dress. Indexed, with bibliography.

R-238 Hulme, E. F. *The History, Principles and Practice of Symbolism in Christian Art.* London, 1909.
Small and of limited use, it provides some of the symbols, signs, and attributes found in Christian subject matter.

R-239 Evans, E. P. *Animal Symbolism in Ecclesiastical Architecture.* New York, 1896.
An old but still serviceable reference in this specialized area.

R-240 Jameson, A. *Sacred and Legendary Art.* Boston, 1896.
A standard, old but not outdated, two-volume commentary on symbols in Christian art, the saints, their emblems and attributes, martyrs, bishops, hermits. Indexed.

R-241 de Bles, A. *How to Distinguish the Saints in Art.* New York, 1925.
Lists the costumes, symbols, attributes, and signs of saints, as well as covering general Christian symbols. Indexed.

R-242 Drake, Maurice and Wilfred. *Saints and Their Emblems.* London, 1916.
An alphabetical listing of Christian saints, as well as some other figures that appear in Christian legend.

R-243 Roeder, H. *Saints and Their Attributes.* London, 1955.
An alphabetical listing of names, attributes, signs, and symbols, with indexes of saints and other holy figures, localities, and patrons. In small format and easy to handle, it includes the manner in which the individuals may be pictured, patronage, instances when saints are invoked, and the costumes of the church. No bibliography.

R-244 Baring-Gould, S. *Lives of the Saints.* London, 1872–1877.
This fifteen-volume production gives more than 3,600 biographies of saints. The listings, however, are by birthdate rather than alphabetical by saint; each volume contains a separate alphabetical listing of its contents. Each entry gives visual symbol or sign of the saint. A very useful reference, but one must first know the birthdate of the saint (see R-243, which is organized alphabetically by saint's name and also provides the birthdates).

R-245 Thurston, H., and D. Attwater, eds. *Butler's Lives of the Saints.* New York, 1956.
A very complete, four-volume revised edition of a standard reference book. It does not give the signs or symbols of the saints, however. A general index is in the last volume, and bibliographies are included with each item.

R-246 Cronin, V., ed. *A Calendar of Saints.* Westminster, 1963.
Alphabetical listing of saints' days, and, therefore, not a complete listing of all such holy figures. Not too useful for biographies of saints, but a picture of each figure is included.

R-247 Kaftal, G. *Iconography of the Saints.* Florence, 1952—.
This volume is concerned with the holy figures represented in Italian painting, and each area in Italian art has a separate volume. Alphabetical listing of saints examines the works of art in which they are represented, and how they are portrayed. Lavishly illustrated, bibliographies for each entry, plus an index of attributes, signs, symbols of holy figures, saints, and painters.

R-248 Weiser, F. X. *Handbook of Christian Feasts and Customs.* New York, 1958.
The various feast days of the Christian calendar, their symbols, and a dictionary of terms. Indexed.

R-249 Thompson, N. and R. Stock. *Complete Concordance to the Bible (Douay Version).* London, 1953.

R-250 Bullinger, E. W. *A Critical Lexicon and Concordance to the English and Greek New Testament.* London, 1957.

R-251 Elder, E., ed. *Concordance to the New English Bible, New Testament.* Grand Rapids, 1964.

R-252 Cruden, A. *A Complete Concordance to the Holy Scriptures of the Old and New Testament (to Which is Added a Concordance to the Books Called Apocrypha).* New York, 1823.

R-253 Ginzberg, L. *Legends of the Jews.*
The stories and legends of the Jewish people retold in several volumes.

R-254 Goodenough, E. *Jewish Symbols in the Greco-Roman Period.* New York, 1953–1968.
Although restricted to ancient art, this thirteen-volume study is the only extensive work on Jewish symbols and provides a basis for the later use of symbols in Jewish and Christian art of the Middle Ages and Renaissance. Index in the last volume.

R-255 *Encyclopedia of Islam.* London, 1954—.
This new edition of an older work is the best reference in the area. In progress.

R-256 Hackin, J., ed. *Asiatic Mythology.* London, 1932.
Mythologies of all the great nations of Asia (Persians, Kafirs, Buddhists, Brahmans, Lamas, Indo-Chinese, Javanese, Hindus, Vedic, Chams, Khmers, Central Asians, Chinese, Shintos, Japanese). Indexed, with illustrations.

R-257 Müller, M., ed. *The Sacred Books of the East.* Oxford, 1879–1910.
The most comprehensive survey of the religious literature of the Orient in forty-nine volumes plus a fiftieth volume which is an index to names and subject.

R-258 Eliot, Charles. *Hinduism and Buddhism.* London, 1921.
A very good history of religion in India and affiliated lands in three volumes.

R-259 Malalesekera, G. P., ed. *Encyclopaedia of Buddhism.* Colombo, 1961—.
An ongoing, excellent reference.

R-260 Getty, A. *The Gods of Northern Buddhism.* Oxford, 1928.
Buddhist lore and iconography. Illustrated, indexed, and with bibliography.

R-261 Nyanatiloka. *Buddhist Dictionary, Manual of Buddhist Terms and Doctrines.* Colombo, 1956.
Composed in short dictionary format, it is useful mainly for religious terms employed in Buddhism.

R-262 Bhattacharyya, B. *The Indian Buddhist Iconography.* Calcutta, 1956.
Unusually complete guide, with illustrated material on signs, symbols, and gods that appear in Buddhist art.

R-263 Dowson, J. *A Classical Dictionary of Hindu Mythology and Religion, Geography, History, and Literature.* London, 1953.
In addition to the material mentioned in the title, it contains a general and a Sanskrit index. A short-entry, small volume, it is very useful for locating symbols, gods, names, and places associated with Oriental art.

R-264 Banerjea, J. N. *The Development of Hindu Iconography.* Calcutta, 1956.
A comprehensive reference on Hindu iconography.

R-265 Thomas, Paul. *Epics, Myths and Legends of India.* Bombay, n.d.
Issued in several editions, the book deals with Hindu and Buddhist gods, legends, stories, fables, tales, etc., presented in a running, narrative format rather than in dictionary entries. Well illustrated for this type of book. It includes a glossary of terms and index.

R-266 Werner, E. T. C. *A Dictionary of Chinese Mythology.* Shanghai, 1932.
A "Who's-Who" of the Chinese otherworld. Provides the Chinese characters after the Latin character entries, in alphabetical order. Added is an index to myths and Chinese terms.

R-267 Williams, C. A. S. *Encyclopaedia of Chinese Symbolism and Art Motives.* New York, 1960.
The volume was first issued (Shanghai, 1941) under the title *Outlines of Chinese Symbolism.*

R-268 Saunders, E. D. *Mudrā: a Study of Symbolic Gestures in Japanese Buddhist Sculpture.* Princeton, 1960.
Hand postures—their histories and meanings. Illustrated.

GENERAL BOOKS AND SERIES ON THE HISTORY OF ART

A very select group of books on different aspects of the history of art appears in this section. They are offered as a compact reading list for the beginner or nonstudent who needs at least a basic recommendation in any one broad segment of the history of art. Hence, while they are useful for advanced study (except for the general survey books), they can also be read by, and are written at an appropriate level for, the general reader. All contain bibliographies which will lead the reader, should he wish to go farther, into the more detailed literature in the area.

General Surveys of Art History. A survey volume on art history usually attempts to provide a continuous narrative over a broad period of time and a number of lands through a careful selection of works of art that the author feels best characterizes the greatest art achievements of man. The survey may attempt to encompass the entire history of art from cave painting to mixed media around the world, or it may survey the same time span in only one land. Less generalized surveys may cover only a principal period (for instance, Italian Renaissance), or a major "School" (Venetian painting), or the lengthy career of a single artist (Michelangelo), or a single style (Mannerism). Some surveys are restricted by medium (surveys of mosaics, or ivory carvings, or manuscript miniatures), while others are limited by frameworks not part of artistic activity but which determine the nature of art (religious art, children's art, ghetto art, social protest art, erotic art).

Whereas the practice many years ago in art history was for a single author to write multivolumed surveys, the more recent publishing policy is to compose an art history survey in a single volume that will be attractive to the general reader and also useful as an introductory textbook at the college level. Another publishing practice is for an editor or editorial board to commission a coordinated series of volumes, each by a specialist in the subject treated in each volume, which can be read separately but which comprise a full survey in the aggregate. Regardless of the number of volumes or size of a survey of art history, it can only cover a small portion of the history of art that is known. In this sense, all survey books are superficial (they can cover only a selected number of matters and items that are considered as absolutely critical and little else), but that fact in no way impairs their value if they are used as introductory books to a very complex and extensive field.

Because the author of a survey tries to present only a broad, panoramic view, the survey is an excellent starting point in one's reading. A grasp of the broad historical situation and the characteristics of the significant styles as expressed in monuments and works is essential before one can concentrate on any single aspect. No two historians, however, are in complete agreement as to what constitutes the most significant, the most critical, or the most valuable artists, works, schools, or styles. Any survey of art history surely must contain the name of Phidias in the discussion of Greek art, but is the same true for his contemporary Scopas? The writer of the survey must compress some of the greatest events and careers of the past into a phrase, while not even mentioning others in the interests of brevity. No survey author is ever satisfied with his finished book: he more than anyone else is painfully aware of how much he had to omit and compress because of practical considerations.

The survey volume is also useful, besides providing easy access into the reading in art history, as a handy reference source. It is a convenient place to locate dates of a major artist, work of art, or monument; to identify the general characteristics of a period or style; or to find identifying illustrations of some major works. Most surveys carry helpful maps, chronological charts, or glossaries of art terms.

Because of the rapidly increasing popularity of art history in college studies, there continues to be a steady supply of general survey texts. The ones listed here are among the most popular for use in beginning art history courses. The list does not pretend to completeness. Not included here are many introductory books of early vintage, since they have limited use today because of their outdated points of view, bulkiness, inadequate illustrations, and lack of coverage of the great gains made in scholarship since they were published.

Because the books cited here are classroom texts first, and volumes for general reading second, their publishers are constantly updating them in new editions to make them better teaching instruments. The publication dates given here may be superseded by later editions, and the latest edition of any of the survey books is the best volume to read. The books are listed from the more general to the more restricted in coverage.

H-269 Cleaver, D. G. *Art: an Introduction.* New York, 1966.
A very brief survey of the Western world, from Egypt to the present, presented in a semi-outline format. The text is keyed to specific objects and artists to typify periods and styles. An inexpensive paperback with small text illustrations, it is indexed and contains a bibliography.

H-270 *Helen Gardner's Art Through the Ages.* New York, 1970.
This has been a standard college text since its appearance in 1926. The latest edition has been thoroughly revised from the previous (1959) one, providing an excellent survey from earliest times to the present. This remains perhaps the best survey text at the college level. Well illustrated, with index and bibliographies.

H-271 Gombrich, E. H. *The Story of Art.* New York, 1956.
An account of art and its content through the ages. Somewhat too simplified and too brief for a college text, it serves as an excellent, easy-to-read narrative. Illustrated, with glossary and bibliography.

H-272 Myers, B. S. *Art and Civilization.* New York, 1967.
A college-level survey text chiefly covering Western art with but a brief mention (less than twenty-five pages) of the Oriental world. Factual, readable, with many good illustrations, bibliography, glossary, and index.

H-273 Janson, H. W. *History of Art.* New York, 1962.
A profusely illustrated (848 black-and-white, seventy-nine full color) college-level history of Western art. A brief postscript deals with the non-Western tradition. The twentieth century is given only a brief mention. Indexed; a helpful listing of books for further reading is divided according to chapters.

H-274 Hauser, Arnold. *The Social History of Art.* London, 1951.
A two-volume specialized approach that stresses social forces as prime determinants of the nature and development of art. Very useful for placing the arts in their cultural context, but the reader must remain aware that this discussion is based on one point of view. The book is excellent in showing how art is part of its environment. One drawback is that some of the sources on which the work depends for its interpretations are rather dated (as can be seen in the bibliographical notes). It contains a small selection of illustrations and is now available in paperback (1957).

H-275 Robb, D. M. and J. J. Garrison. *Art in the Western World.* New York, 1963.
College survey text divided into four parts according to art form: architecture, sculpture, painting, and the minor arts. It covers periods from the earliest times to the present in the West. Small text illustrations, bibliography, glossary, and index.

H-276 Upjohn, E. M., P. S. Wingert, and J. G. Mahler. *History of World Art.* Oxford, 1956.
College text of both Western and Oriental art. Small but good illustrations placed together at the front of the book in the 1948 edition are handled more easily in the revised edition and are placed throughout the text. Bibliography, glossary, and index.

H-277 Faure, E. *History of Art.* New York, 1921–1930.
Not intended as a textbook, the five-volume history forms a spirited retelling of the story of art throughout history in the East and West. The author captures the spirit and climate of the arts and views the panoramic sweep of history with sensitivity and sophistication.

H-278 Bazin, G. *History of Art.* London, 1958.
A survey of both East and West in one volume, with small illustrations not coordinated with the text. Bibliography and index.

H-279 Sewall, J. I. *A History of Western Art.* New York, 1961.
A college survey book with primary emphasis on architecture. This revised edition (1961) adds a final chapter on modern art written by John Canaday. Helpful appendices on architectural principals and color theory; black-and-white illustrations only. Indexed, but no bibliography or reading lists.

H-280 Levey, M. *History of Western Art.* London, 1968.
A personalized, enthusiastic accounting of Western art for adult readers. The organization is difficult to follow. No reading suggestions.

H-281 Pevsner, N. *An Outline of European Architecture.* Harmondsworth, 1960.
A brief, authoritative treatment within the limits of a single-volume survey. Good illustrations.

H-282 Hamlin, T. *Architecture through the Ages.* New York, 1953.
A college-level survey dealing with Western architecture from earliest times to the present, with brief excursus on Islamic and Far Eastern. Small text illustrations, indexed, but no reading suggestions.

H-283 Robb, D. M. *The Harper History of Painting, the Occidental Tradition.* New York, 1951.
Restricted to the field of painting in Europe and America, with bibliography, glossary, and index.

H-284 Pope-Hennessey, J., ed. *A History of Western Sculpture.*
A four-volume work divided and authored as follows: *1*—G. M. A. Hanfmann, *Classical Sculpture; 2*—R. Salvini, *Medieval Sculpture; 3*—H. Keutner, *Sculpture: Renaissance and Baroque; 4*—F. S. Licht, *Sculpture: Nineteenth and Twentieth Century.*

H-285 Mendelowitz, D. M. *Drawing.* New York, 1967.
A large book that discusses media, techniques, and elements of drawing, but useful here for the first section devoted to the history of drawing. Many excellent illustrations, select bibliography, and index.

Art History Series. Many publishing houses produce coordinated series of art history books. Each volume is usually self-contained and can be used profitably without reference to other volumes in the series. Listed here are some of the best series in terms of scholarship and others which are less scholarly but have compensating features, such as excellent illustrations. Some foreign language series are cited because of their importance in art history research.

H-286 *Pelican History of Art.* Harmondsworth.
Produced in England, this represents the best comprehensive series on art and architecture in English, to be completed in forty-eight volumes. Each volume is written by a major scholar (or scholars), is heavily illustrated, is documented, and has excellent bibliographies. The texts are scholarly written, not for general leisure reading, but well suited for undergraduates as well as graduate students and professionals. Among the titles already published are works on the art and architecture of India, Britain, Russia, ancient Near East, ancient Egypt, Belgium, Italy, Japan, Greece, Carolingian and Romanesque Europe, the nineteenth and twentieth centuries.

H-287 *Propyläen Kunstgeschichte* (New edition). Berlin.
One of the standard scholarly reference series for world art published by the Propyläen publishers in the 1920s and 1930s is being reissued in an entirely rewritten edition that will contain eighteen volumes. Each volume is heavily illustrated and has ample documentation and lucid text. The completed series will include: Greeks and their neighbors, Roman Empire, Byzantine and Christian East, Carolingian and Romanesque, middle ages, Islam, Renaissance, Baroque, Mannerism, Rococo and Classicism, nineteenth century, modern, prehistory, old Orient, India and Southeast Asia, China and Japan, Amerindian, Egyptian (in German).

H-288 *Praeger World of Art.* New York.
Praeger, publisher of fine art books, has this very good, well illustrated series of handbooks written by recognized authorities. The volumes are very useful for undergraduate student

work. While not specialized, they provide concise surveys. Individual volumes vary greatly in coverage and area as the following list illustrates: ancient art of the Americas; ancient art of Central Asia; art of the ancient Near East; art of the Byzantine Era; Baroque and Rococo Art; English painting; modern sculpture; painting from Giotto to Cézanne; Paul Klee; Henry Moore; George Seurat.

H-289 *Contact History of Art.* London.
A series of small handbooks, very serviceable, with abbreviated texts and a generous selection of illustrations. The series is put out in the United States as the *Compass History of Art.* The volumes on the history of painting include Greek, Roman, Etruscan, early Christian, Byzantine, medieval, Manuscript, Renaissance, seventeenth century, eighteenth century, nineteenth century, and twentieth century.

H-290 *Arts of Mankind.* London.
The English edition of this sumptuous French series is published by Thames and Hudson. Each volume is lavishly illustrated, written by outstanding scholars, and contains annotations of photographs, bibliographies, glossary, and maps. The first seven volumes cover the ancient lands of Sumer, Assyria, Iran, Parthia, Sasania, Greece, the South Pacific, and Italy of the Renaissance.

H-291 Cossió, M. B. and J. Pijoân. *Summa Artis.* Bilbao-Madrid.
A comprehensive history of the art of all cultures. Begun in 1931, the project is still in progress. Well illustrated; contains bibliographies (in Spanish).

H-292 Burger, F. and A. E. Brinckmann. *Handbuch der Kunstwissenschaft.* Berlin.
A world history published between 1913–1930, comprising twenty-seven volumes (in German).

H-293 Michel, A. *Histoire de l'art depuis les premiers temps chrétiens jusqu'à nos jours.* Paris.
An early French series (1905–1929) in seventeen volumes, plus an index (in French).

H-294 *Ancient Peoples and Places.* London.
An excellent series published by Thames and Hudson (London) on the art and archaeology of the ancient world. Each volume, by an acknowledged expert, is concisely written and very well illustrated. The high caliber of the series is not diminished by the fact that the text is written without highly technical minutiae. More than forty volumes have appeared covering such areas as underwater archaeology, India and Pakistan, Colombia, Medes and Persians, Mycenaeans, Etruscans, Egyptians, Byzantines, Canaanites, Greeks, early Christian, Seljuks, Poland, South Africa, Vikings.

H-295 *Great Art and Artists of the World Series.* New York.
Each volume provides a popular historical introduction for the many illustrations in color and black-and-white. Generally, the volumes are useful for their broad survey and as a "who's who" of the most famous artists. Sample volumes are Italian art to 1850, Flemish and Dutch art, Impressionists and post-Impressionists, Chinese and Japanese art, and modern art.

H-296 *Skira Art Books: Painting-Color-History.* Geneva.
The Skira Publishers are noted for their handsomely produced, luxuriously illustrated volumes with English texts. The usefulness of the texts varies from volume to volume. Among the subjects covered in this series are the following: Dutch, Flemish, French, German, Italian, Spanish, and modern painting. While these volumes can be used to advantage for their excellent, sometimes over-brilliant reproductions and for providing a broad survey of painting, they are not designed for intensive study.

H-297 *The Great Centuries of Painting.* Geneva.
Another Skira publishing house survey, excellently illustrated, and written by respected scholars for the lay audience. Included are the paintings of Lascaux, Egypt, Greece, Etruria, Rome, Byzantium, the Middle Ages, and the fifteenth through the nineteenth centuries.

H-298 *The Taste of Our Time.* Geneva.
A popular Skira series on contemporary individual art movements and great masters, with good quality color illustrations. Represented in more than forty volumes are, for example, Botticelli, Carpaccio, Chagall, Dufy, Fra Angelico, Gauguin, Kandinsky, Miro, Rembrandt, Vermeer, Cubism, Fauvism, Impressionism, Romanticism, Surrealism.

H-299 *Treasures of Asia.* Geneva.
A series in English, edited by the Skira publishing house, on Oriental painting with the usual high quality of book production of this company. Six volumes include the painting of China, Persia, Japan, India, Central Asia, and the Arab world.

H-300 *Treasures of the World.* Geneva.
Not intended to be comprehensive in coverage, this beautifully produced and illustrated series, by Skira, reviews the history of art as seen in some of the most handsome examples in, for example, ancient America, Spain, Turkey, Venice, and the Vatican.

H-301 *UNESCO World Art Series.* New York.
Published by the New York Graphic Society for UNESCO, this series of large format picture books has excellent, large illustrations in color, introduced by short, usually well written essays. Each volume deals with one representative aspect of a nation's art, for instance: India—the Ajanta cave paintings; Rumania—church paintings in Moldavia; Cyprus—Byzantine murals; USSR—icons; Turkey—manuscript miniatures; Australia—aboriginal painting; Iran—miniatures; Israel—ancient mosaics; Bulgaria—Medieval wall paintings; Norway—stave church painting.

H-302 Venturi, A. *Storia dell'arte italiana.* Milan.
Eleven volumes (in twenty-five parts) compose this series, published between 1909 and 1940. Well indexed and containing more than 18,000 illustrations, it covers Italian art and architecture from prehistory through the sixteenth century (in Italian).

H-303 Janson, H. W., ed. *Sources and Documents in the History of Art Series.* Englewood Cliffs.
A series of paperback volumes published by Prentice-Hall that provides selections of original source material—letters, articles, diaries, histories, reviews—translated into English. Cogent prefatory remarks introduce the materials in each book. Not illustrated, and some volumes not indexed. Each book deals with a specific period or culture, for example, art of America (1700–1960), Greece (1400–31 B.C.), Northern Renaissance (1400–1600), and Italy (1500–1600).

H-304 *Corpus Vitrearum Medii Aevi.*
This is a catalog-type publication that is being produced for different art forms on an international scale. Under the aegis of an international committee, scholars in each nation produce complete catalogs of the medieval stained glass in their lands. A single volume may cover the entire country, or, in the case of France, for example, where there are rich remains, may cover only a group of monuments or a region. Each volume in the series is published in the language of national origin. Another such catalog series, for example, is that which aims eventually to be a complete catalog of ancient Greek vases *(Corpus Vasorum Antiquorum).*

General Periods and Countries. A brief selection of general texts on the several broad areas encompassed in the study of art history follows. To select one or two books in each classification is to court disaster: no two students of art history would agree on the choice of a single most recommended book; concensus on an entire list or even the areas that should be selected would be impossible. However, the books which follow are standard, commonly used, and recommended as readable introductions that provide comprehensive summaries. These books are listed only to provide a broad reference and a point of departure for further reading. They may not be in every case the best possible books, but they are among the most useful and most easily obtainable.

Western Art

H-305 (prehistoric)
Graziosi, P. *Paleolithic Art.* New York, 1960.

H-306 (prehistoric)
Leroi-Gourhan, A. *Treasures of Prehistoric Art.* New York, 1967.

H-307 (ancient painting)
Swindler, M. H. *Ancient Painting.* New Haven, 1929.

H-308 (ancient Mediterranean)
Matz, F. *The Art of Crete and Early Greece.* New York, 1962.

H-309 (Greek)
Richter, G. M. A. *A Handbook of Greek Art.* London, 1967.

H-310 (Greek)
Lawrence, A. W. *Greek Architecture.* Baltimore, 1957.

H-311 (Greek)
Robertson, Martin. *Greek Painting.* New York, 1959.

H-312 (Greek)
Richter, G. M. A. *The Sculpture and Sculptors of the Greeks.* New Haven, 1950.

H-313 (Roman)
Kähler, H. *Rome and Her Empire.* New York, 1963.

H-314 (early Christian)
Volbach, W. F. and M. Hirmer. *Early Christian Art.* London, 1960.

H-315 (migration)
Hubert, J., J. Porcher, W. F. Volbach. *Europe of the Invasions.* New York, 1969.

H-316 (Byzantine)
Rice, D. T. *The Art of Byzantium.* New York, 1959.

H-317 (Byzantine)
Dalton, O. M. *Byzantine Art and Archaeology.* Oxford, 1911.

H-318 (Medieval)
Morey, C. R. *Medieval Art.* New York, 1942.

H-319 (Medieval)
Porter, A. K. *Medieval Architecture.* New Haven, 1912, 2 vols.

H-320 (Medieval)
Grabar, A. and Nordenfalk K. *Early Medieval Painting.* Geneva, 1957.

H-321 (Medieval)
Focillon, H. *Art of the West in the Middle Ages.* New York, 1962, 2 vols.

H-322 (Renaissance, North)
Panofsky, E. *Early Netherlandish Painting.* Cambridge, Mass., 1954, 2 vols.

H-323 (Renaissance, North)
Benesch, O. *The Art of the Renaissance in Northern Europe.* Cambridge, Mass., 1945.

H-324 (Renaissance, South)
Wölfflin, H. *Principles of Art History.* London, 1932.

H-325 (Renaissance, South)
Anderson, W. J. *The Architecture of the Renaissance in Italy.* New York, 1927.

H-326 (Renaissance, South)
Pope-Hennessy, J. W. *An Introduction to Italian Sculpture.* New York, 1955–1963, 5 vols.

H-327 (Baroque)
Wittkower, R. *Art and Architecture in Italy, 1600–1750.* Baltimore, 1958.

H-328 (Baroque)
Wittkower, R. *Architectural Principles in the Age of Humanism.* New York, 1966.

H-329 (Baroque)
Bazin, G. *Baroque and Rococo Art.* New York, 1965.

H-330 (Baroque)
Maclagan, E. R. D. *Italian Sculpture of the Renaissance.* Cambridge, Mass., 1935.

H-331 (Rococo)
Schonberger, A. and H. Soehner, *The Age of the Rococo.* London, 1960.

H-332 (nineteenth century)
Hitchcock, H.-R. *Architecture, Nineteenth and Twentieth Centuries.* Baltimore, 1958.

H-333 (nineteenth century)
Canaday, J. *Mainstreams of Modern Art.* New York, 1959.

H-334 (twentieth century)
Grohmann, W. *New Art Around the World.* New York, 1966.

H-335 (twentieth century)
Giedion, S. *Space, Time, and Architecture.* Cambridge, Mass., 1941.

H-336 (twentieth century)
Haftmann, W. *Painting in the Twentieth Century.* New York, 1965, 2 vols.

H-337 (twentieth century)
Giedion-Welcker, C. *Contemporary Sculpture.* New York, 1955.

H-338 (American)
Larkin, Oliver. *Art and Life in America.* New York, 1949.

H-339 (American)
Garrett, W. D., P. F. Norton, A. Gowans, and J. T. Butler. *The Arts in America: the 19th Century.* New York, 1969.

H-340 (American)
Richardson, E. P. *Painting in America.* New York, 1956.

H-341 (American)
Gardner, A. T. E. *American Sculpture.* Greenwich, 1964.

Non-Western Art

H-342 (Far East)
Lee, Sherman. *A History of Far Eastern Art.* New York, 1964.

H-343 (Far East)
Swann, P. *The Art of China, Korea, and Japan.* New York, 1963.

H-344 (India)
Rowland, B. *The Art and Architecture of India: Buddhist, Hindu, Jain.* Baltimore, 1953.

H-345 (India)
Zimmer, H. *The Art of Indian Asia.* New York, 1955, 2 vols.

H-346 (Islamic)
Dimand, M. S. *Handbook of Muhammaden Art.* New York, 1947.

H-347 (Islamic)
Rice, D. T. *Islamic Art.* New York, 1965.

H-348 (Egyptian)
Aldred, C. *Art in Ancient Egypt.* London, 1952.

H-349 (Egyptian)
Lange, K. and M. Hirmer. *Egypt: Architecture, Sculpture, Painting in Three Thousand Years.* New York, 1956.

H-350 (Near East)
Frankfort, H. *Art and Architecture of the Ancient Orient.* Baltimore, 1955.

H-351 (Near East)
Lloyd, Seton. *Art of the Ancient Near East.* New York, 1961.

H-352 (African)
Leuzinger, E. *Africa: The Art of the Negro Peoples.* New York, 1960.

H-353 (African)
Leiris, M. and J. Delange. *African Art.* London, 1968.

H-354 (African)
Wingert, P. S. *The Sculpture of Negro Africa.* New York, 1950.

H-355 (African)
Locke, A. *The Negro in Art.* New York, 1940.

H-356 (Oceana)
Linton, R., and P. S. Wingert. *Arts of the South Seas.* New York, 1946.

H-357 (Oceana)
Christensen, E. O. *Primitive Art.* New York, 1955.

H-358 (Amerindian)
Vaillant, G. *Indian Arts in North America.* New York, 1939.

H-359 (Amerindian)
Douglas, F. H. and R. d'Harnoncourt. *Indian Art of the United States.* New York, 1941.

H-360 (Amerindian)
Kelemen, P. *Medieval American Art.* New York, 1943, 2 vols.

H-361 (Amerindian)
Dockstader, F. J. *Indian Art of Middle America.* Greenwich, 1964.

H-362 (folk art)
Bossert, H. T. *Folk Art of Europe; Folk Art of Asia, Africa, and the Americas; Folk Art of Primitive Peoples.* New York, 1964, 3 vols.

H-363 (esthetics)
Gilbert, K. A., and H. Kuhn. *A History of Aesthetics.* Indiana, 1953.

H-364 (esthetics)
Rader, M., ed. *A Modern Book of Esthetics.* New York, 1960.

ART HISTORY AND ART PERIODICALS

Articles concerned directly or indirectly with the arts appear in a wide variety of magazines and journals—historical, religious, anthropological, archaeological, etc. There also are many professional and popular periodicals that are devoted entirely to the visual arts, ranging from scholarly studies to art news reporting. Journal articles are essential reading for most research because new discoveries, insights, and analyses most often first appear in this form. Some of the most vital, penetrating scholarly writing appears in journal articles and then later is incorporated into books.

We can separate periodical publications dealing with the arts into three broad categories: 1) journals which publish professional, scholarly studies in the history of art only; 2) journals which contain articles written by competent scholars for the professional field and the interested layman, the intelligent amateur, and the collector; 3) magazines which are designed to bring to the art enthusiast, the art student, and the general public news of current art activities and of the personalities who are making the art news. The first type of publication is basic to reading in art history, the second type must be used selectively, and the third type, while useful in keeping up-to-date with the contemporary scene, rarely is sufficient for study and analysis.

There is no universal index of articles that appear in all journals published around the world, and, hence, there is always some difficulty in discovering what has been written and where it appeared. However, the *Art Index* (B-17) notes many of the major art publications.

Listed here is a selection of periodicals in each of these three categories that are printed in the English language or that sometimes contain English language articles or summaries in English of articles in other languages. There are dozens of foreign language journals that are essential in the study of art history, but they are excluded here because of their language.

Professional Periodicals. Articles appearing in the following journals will have been professionally screened, offering maximum assurance of their accuracy and importance as new contributions in the study of art history.

J-365 *The Art Bulletin. New York.* Published quarterly by the College Art Association, which is the professional society of American art historians and collegiate studio art teachers, its contents cover the entire range of art history but concentrate on Western European. A lengthy book review section is an important feature. The first twenty-one volumes (1913–1948) have been indexed in a separate volume (1950).

J-366 *The Art Quarterly.* Detroit.
This journal and the *Art Bulletin* are the two primary professional journals published in the United States that are generally concerned with the broad field of Western art. Extremely valuable are its listings of recent accessions by United States and Canadian museums, its reviews of major exhibitions, and the extensive book reviews.

J-367 *Apollo.* London.
A scholarly journal published monthly for collectors and connoisseurs. Handsomely illustrated short articles are supplemented with a very extensive coverage of gallery announcements and advertisements on an international level.

J-368 *The Burlington Magazine.* London.
One of the chief English-language art historical and critical periodicals of international reputation, now appearing monthly. The well annotated articles are supplemented with book reviews, extensive advertising that covers current gallery exhibitions, and lists of major shows. A separate index volume covering the first 104 volumes was published in 1962.

J-369 *Journal of the Warburg and Courtauld Institutes.* London.
A quarterly published by one of the chief art history training and research centers. It emphasizes iconographical studies of Western European art.

J-370 *Gazette des Beaux-Arts.* Paris.
One of the most venerable of art journals, its publishing history goes back to 1859. It now has an international board of editors, contains some articles in the English language, and frequently provides English summaries for the French articles. Usually published monthly, it is additionally valuable for a supplement *(La Chronique des arts)* that provides current news of exhibitions, personalities in the arts, conferences, books, and articles.

J-371 *Pantheon.* Munich.
A monthly international art journal that is concerned with all periods, mainly in German, but also containing English language articles. Its scholarly, documented essays are supplemented with book reviews and news of museum events.

J-372 *Oud Holland.* Amsterdam.
A quarterly primarily publishing articles on Netherlandish art, some written in English.

J-373 *Journal of the Archives of American Art.* Detroit.
This relatively new, slender quarterly is chiefly concerned with publishing articles dealing with the archival material held by its sponsoring organization, the Archives of American Art. Hence, its contents deal only with American artists and arts, providing a good deal of primary source material.

J-374 *Antike Kunst.* Olten.
A Swiss journal of international proportions that publishes chiefly in the field of the Classical arts, in English, French, and German.

J-375 *American Journal of Archaeology.* New York.
The quarterly publication of the Archaeological Institute of America is primarily for studies and reports on the ancient Mediterranean world and the adjacent regions. Thus, it is particularly important for research in Greek and Roman art.

It contains an extensive coverage of publications in its review section and maintains running reports of discoveries of ancient monuments.

J-376 *Artibus Asiae.* New York.
Specializing in the arts of the Orient and Western Asia, this international journal is designed for scholars and connoisseurs. The articles are chiefly in English (except for the earlier volumes).

J-377 *Ars Orientalis.* Washington.
A very large single issue of high scholarly quality, is published every other year on the arts of Eastern and Western Asia. It is the continuation of the previously published *Ars Islamica,* which chiefly focused on the Islamic arts.

J-378 *Oriental Art.* London.
A quarterly carrying short but authoritative articles for students, collectors, and intelligent amateurs of Far Eastern art. It is additionally useful for exhibition and sales notices and for bibliographies of books and articles on Oriental art.

J-379 *Master Drawings.* New York.
Recently inaugurated, this quarterly is devoted exclusively to the scholarly, documentary, and historical studies of drawings of the "master" painters.

J-380 *Journal of the Society of Architectural Historians.* Philadelphia.
A quarterly, sponsored by the professional society of architectural historians in the United States, that covers architectural studies of all periods and includes short reviews.

J-381 *Journal of Aesthetics and Art Criticism.* Cleveland/Detroit.
The scholarly, quarterly publication of the American Society for Aesthetics covers all branches of the theoretical and critical aspects of the several arts.

J-382 *Marsyas.* New York.
A publication by the graduate students of the New York Institute of Fine Arts, it covers all areas of art history and also provides a list of theses and summaries of dissertations

submitted to the faculty of this major center for the training of art historians.

Journals on the Arts. The following selection of periodicals is usually at a professional level of authorship, but written with the general reader in mind.

J-383 *Art Journal (College Art Journal).* New York.
The popular publication on the arts and artists of the College Art Association (whose scholarly publication is the *College Art Bulletin*) appears quarterly. It contains short, informative articles, usually on current topics. It is handy for keeping up with the art activities of the colleges and galleries. It serves as a forum for discussions of contemporary interest to the collegiate art world, contains news columns on personalities and personnel in museums and colleges, and lists collections, exhibitions, gallery shows, and titles of doctoral dissertations in process and completed.

J-384 *American Art Journal.* New York.
A recent arrival in the art journal field is this twice-yearly publication concerned with the history of American art and written for the intelligent layman and collector.

J-385 *African Arts.* Los Angeles.
A new quarterly devoted to general cultural essays on the graphic, plastic, literary, and performing arts of Africa. The extensive pictorial coverage is particularly helpful.

J-386 *Archaeology.* New York.
A popular quarterly for the interested amateur of ancient art and archaeology, with articles written by the specialists who are themselves uncovering the treasures of the past; hence, it is authoritative. Published by the Archaeological Institute of America, along with its scholarly *American Journal of Archaeology.*

J-387 *Bollettino d'art.* Rome
At first a monthly, but now a quarterly, this journal carries scholarly materials on Italian art with important current notices of activities in the arts and museums of Italy.

Although it does not publish in English, it is included here because of its usefulness in one of the most popular areas in the study of the arts (in Italian).

J-388 *La Critica d'arte.* Florence.
While mainly written in Italian, some of the professional level articles are in English. A bimonthly, it is primarily concerned with Italian art.

J-389 *The Connoisseur.* London.
A monthly magazine for the art and antique collector published since the beginning of this century, it carries extensive gallery advertisements and notices of antique auctions and sales.

J-390 *Print.* New York.
A bimonthly magazine for industrial, commercial, and graphic design printing, it is of major interest to people working in the field.

J-391 *Museum News.* Wisconsin.
The official newsletter of the American Association of Museums, it is published bimonthly. Primarily for people in museum and museology programs.

J-392 *Museums Journal.* London.
The monthly publication of the Museums Association, it carries articles and reports on the management, activities, and business of museums and museum personnel.

J-393 *Museum.*
The successor to *Mouseion,* a UNESCO publication that carries quarterly reports of museum works and studies at an international level.

Popular Arts Magazines. Out of the great number of popular magazines on the arts, the following few are the most representative. They are mostly for general art public, those interested in what is happening in studios and galleries now, in the current events in the lives of contemporary artists and art movements, and in the tastes and doings of art dealers and collectors. The short articles and essays have a journalistic bias, but the gallery and dealers' advertisements are useful in indicating what is happening in the modern art centers.

J-394 *Art News.* New York.
Published ten times a year for artists, art students, and art enthusiasts.

J-395 *Art International.* Zurich.
Up-to-the-minute reportings on the art world, issued ten times a year.

J-396 *Art in America.* New York.
A bimonthly for experienced art amateurs and collectors of the contemporary.

J-397 *Arts Magazine.* New York.
Published eight times a year, it mainly covers the current New York scene.

J-398 *Arts Canada.* Toronto.
The Canadian bimonthly for art enthusiasts.

J-399 *Canadian Art.* Ottawa.
A quarterly review of the contemporary arts in Canada.

J-400 *Studio International.* London.
Popular articles on modern art, appearing eleven times a year.

J-401 *Liturgical Arts.* Concord.
A Catholic quarterly for the contemporary arts and artists of the Church.

J-402 *National Sculpture.*
A popular trade magazine for the practicing sculptor and amateur (non-avant garde), published by the National Sculpture Society.

J-403 *Graphis.*
A bimonthly, trilingual (English, French, German) journal for the modern graphic and applied arts.

4

Research and Writing in the History of Art

WRITING A RESEARCH PAPER

STUDY of the history of art at the college level usually includes library and museum research leading to a documented essay. It is a rare student who enters an art history class without having had some experience at research paper writing and who has not dealt with card catalogs, footnotes, bibliographies, and the other apparatus of scholarly writing. English composition textbooks usually take upon themselves the responsibility for outlining the form and format of research paper writing. Thus, this section does not pretend to provide an elaborate description of the practices and techniques of scholarly research and writing. Rather, it reviews some of the basic points and offers suggestions on those techniques of reading and writing that particularly affect the study of art history.

The undergraduate research paper in art history will seldom produce a startling new discovery; nevertheless, it need not be viewed as simply an exercise in restatement or synopsis of what one has read. Although the particular problem the student is working on may have been the subject of study by generations of scholars, the student, approaching it with a fresh eye and mind, and with his contemporary point of view, can make the paper, for himself and for his reader, something more than just another trudge down a well worn path.

The experience of writing a paper offers the student the opportunity to concentrate his attention on a small facet of a large and frequently confusing aspect of cultural history. It offers him the chance to familiarize himself with the literature of the field, to find out what has been written, who the writers are, what is known, and what is unknown or gravely questioned. Yet another purpose of the research paper is to introduce the student to the technique of writing history. Too often we come to the field of history, and art history in particular, with the feeling that the past is not only fully known, but also, like revealed wisdom, beyond doubt—a belief which is profoundly untrue. Art history, a relatively modern discipline, is still being written and rewritten. What we know about the artists and arts of the past is only a small corner of what is yet to be learned; and much that we do know is constantly undergoing reevaluation and correction or confirmation.

The best way to find out how we know what we know about the arts is to try one's hand at writing art history—to go to the basic evidence, evaluate it, synthesize the available information, and then to see what inferences and conclusions, tentative as they may be, can be reasonably drawn. History is not a science; it is a humanistic engagement with man's activities in the past, the drawing of the most reasonable conclusions based upon a logical estimate of the evidence. By reading critically and attempting to write history, the student can discover for himself the uncertainties, frustrations, pitfalls, and pleasures of reconstructing the spiritual adventures of his forebears as they have been concretized in the art object.

There is no single formula for writing a research paper, no single correct procedure or format. Every student develops his own techniques for gathering, remembering, organizing, and writing down the results of his studying. Some students must take copious notes on their readings and analyses of works of art; some students have excellent memories and can rely on skeletal notes. Some students can organize their thoughts in respectable English syntax almost at the first writing, while others need to write and rewrite. Some students prefer to build a paper from an outline, while others find it more helpful to develop the paper first and then go back and outline it to see if the ideas are clear and logically organized.

The several types of subject matter studied in art history demand various approaches. A paper that sets out to document a single work of art makes different demands than one that seeks to analyze a historical style. A paper on, for example, the sculptor Myron, who has left no written documents, will demand a different approach and handling of evidence than a paper on, say, the painter Delacroix, who wrote extensively in journals and letters. But although there are no absolute rules that apply to the composition of *all* research papers, there are some general principles that the student should follow to make the research and writing manageable and profitable.

Selecting a Topic. The general topic will, of course, be determined by the course and instructor, but unless an exact subject is assigned, the student must himself determine the limits of his paper. The first test for a proposed subject is its specificity: is the topic sufficiently specific and well defined to be adequately covered in the amount of time available for research, with the variety of reference materials available, and within the length limits of the paper to be written? Few students err on the side of picking a topic that is too small; most subjects first selected would require the concentrated efforts of an established specialist for many years, to be written down in several volumes. Almost as a rule, students overreach themselves in selecting a topic for a research paper. No one can do justice to a topic such as "The History of American Architecture" in the space of 3,000 words and with three weeks' time for reading. Although within the general history of architecture—a history that covers the globe and over ten thousand years—the story of American architecture may seem small, still it contains thousands of works by almost as many architects of diverse ideas, styles, and backgrounds, covering many decades.

Would the work of one architect be too large or too small a subject for a convenient term research paper? There is no set answer. A short study of the works of a nineteenth-century architect about whom little is known and whose surviving buildings number but few may be nicely treated in a short research paper, even though it may not be an exhaustive study. On the other hand, an attempt to write a short paper on the entire career of Frank Lloyd Wright—a career that spanned several decades, involved the creation of many buildings, led to new and involved architectural approaches and philosophies, and which has been extensively written on by Wright himself and numerous critics and historians—would probably flounder in the sea of material to be read and mastered.

In general, the more specific the subject, the easier it is to control the bibliography, to organize the material, and to arrive at some succinct and clearly defined conclusions.

While it is always more adventuresome to write on some exotic problem or topic in the arts, rather than on a standard one, the student must always be sure that the topic selected is capable of being studied by him. He must ask if there are adequate illustrations of the art objects. Are adequate library materials on the subject available? Is the basic literature available in a language he reads? Has sufficient work already been accomplished on or near the subject to provide a primary list of source readings? There is nothing more discouraging than undertaking research on a subject for which the library has few of the basic books or periodicals, and those it does have are written in Chinese or some other language that the student does not easily handle.

Gathering Source Materials. The student of art history has a certain advantage over students in many other fields. Usually students do not handle primary source material in their college work until they are well along in graduate studies: few English students handle manuscripts, few music students hear the composer play, at least until they have undergone long preparatory training. But the art history student can frequently go directly to his primary source material—the painting, the building, the sculpture—that he is studying; he can examine the tangible object that bears the mark of the artist's hand. Usually he works with photographs, but the availability of local museum, art gallery, collection, or building means that he can experience his material without intervention, even though he and the artist are separated by hundreds or thousands of years. Art objects are the primary source materials for art history research, and hence they should be consulted first in any study and remain basic to all research.

Another type of primary source material is that formed by the literary documents that are contemporaneous with the art work under study. For example, there are the writings of artists: Vincent van Gogh's letters, Louis Sullivan's books, Michelangelo's poems, Leonardo da Vinci's treatises, Wassily Kandinsky's esthetic theories. We have the writings of commentators who are nearly or exactly contemporary with the artist: Vasari's biographies, Gertrude Stein's appreciation of the young Picasso, the poet Rilke's writings on the sculptor Rodin. And there are contemporary official and legal documents:

painting guild records, church contracts for commissions, Assyrian annals. Such primary source material is the backbone of art history research. The student should work with this literature whenever possible, for the more he does, the more interesting, authoritative, and fruitful the results of his study will be. Fortunately for the student today, large quantities of this type of source material, previously difficult to obtain and mostly in foreign tongues, are now easily available in paperback anthologies, unfortunately (but necessarily) heavily edited (see H-303).

A basic rule to follow is: whenever possible go back to the primary source in your reading. Unless unavoidable, because of unavailability or foreign language difficulty, one should never quote one author quoting someone else or an original source. Thus, for example, if an author quotes a statement by the Renaissance biographer-painter Vasari that is particularly useful for a paper, one should refer back to an English translation of Vasari (unless the student can read Italian) rather than use the secondhand quotation. One should never be satisfied with an art historian's quotations from Pliny on Greek art, from Leonardo's treatise on painting, or from van Gogh's letters to his brother. Almost any library of college caliber will have these basic writings in English (and the secondary source being read usually acknowledges the exact location of the original quotation). In the same manner, while one may read with profit the descriptions of works of art by different authors, when at all possible one should go to the work itself (or a satisfactory illustration of it) and make a firsthand, fresh descriptive analysis. It is of prime importance in the history of art to stay as close as possible to the work and to the artist who made it.

Community of Opinion. No matter how creative an author's point of view, no matter how profound his knowledge of the matter under consideration, he must take into account the ideas that are generally held by the community of scholars in the field. This need to be cognizant of the scholarly community of opinion on any one subject is not only necessary for the professional historian but also for the student of art history. As in any field of human study, art history has its different schools of thought, and reputable scholars disagree on basic matters, as well as on minor points. The student must recognize that such differences do exist, and, hence, he must never accept the categorical statement of one author as absolute truth without having checked to see whether that statement represents general opinion or is uniquely held by that one author. The student writer can never hope to restrict his subject to a matter about which all scholars agree (fortunately, for much of the pleasure of working in art history is the challenge of finding that most all matters are controversial). It is only important that in his reading the student attain sufficient breadth to be aware of possible differences of opinions, interpretations, attributions, dates, and classifications. This mandate to be aware of what the community of scholars thinks on any subject does not mean that the most commonly held opinion is the most correct. On the contrary, it may be that the one scholar who disagrees with the community of opinion will be proved to be right, once all the evidence is in and evaluated. The test of scholarship is accuracy, not popularity.

But how does the student just beginning his studies in any branch of art history know what point of view represents the community of opinion? A rule of thumb is never to be satisfied with one source only. After reading a clear exposition or obtaining the facts from one author, the student should check the information in the writings of other writers. If there should be a divergence of opinion or fact, the student may wish to follow one or the other author, but at least he can note the fact that contrary views exist. Obviously, some books or some authors are more authoritative than others in some, if not all, matters. One of the difficulties experienced by the beginning student is an inability to identify which are the sound, widely respected opinions, which are the basic authors, which are the opinions that are little more than guesses, and which are the authors that must be read with great caution. The student usually relies upon his teacher to identify the reliable scholarship in the field, and, thus, one begins with a basic cadre of authors whose writings are respected. But beyond that list the student can proceed with caution, following some general guide lines outlined below.

"Good" and "Bad" Art History Books. Books and articles in art history, like books and articles dealing with any subject, range from profound studies to negligible scribbles. The trained eye can usually

distinguish between these extremes on the basis of internal evidence: the manner of writing, the level of discourse, the manner in which evidence is handled, the amount of data cited, and the critical way in which supporting material is employed. The student, however, usually must rely on the reputation of the author and on comparisons with other texts. Certainly one test of an author's views is the quality of his reputation among his peers. The student should notice which writers are most often found in bibliographies and notes and which authors most often appear in quotations or are cited as the source of information. A scholar who is constantly being referred to by other authors may not always be right, but at least his judgment bears some weight. On the other hand, one must use with extreme caution an author whose name appears nowhere else than in his own writings, despite the fact that the material on which he writes is of great interest to many scholars.

If the student wants to check on the reputation and caliber of scholarship of an author, to discover if he is regarded seriously by his colleagues, he can gain a fairly accurate assessment by looking over book reviews of the author's work. As I will discuss more fully in the paragraphs on book reviews, reviews must be read with care. But if the book is reviewed in a respectable journal, if the reviewer himself has published in the field, and if the reviewer treats the book with care and attention, then there is reason to respect the writings of the author. That is not to say that the review must always be enthusiastic; the reviewer and author may argue over many matters, but it is the seriousness with which the reviewer treats the book that is an index to its worth.

Should the source material in question be in a journal or magazine, the student has another index for determining its reliability. What kind of journal has printed the article? Is it a serious or scholarly publication, or is it a pulp magazine? Is the journal or magazine seriously concerned with the history of art, or is it a magazine that is merely "arty?"

One means of estimating the reliability of an author requires careful, discriminating reading, a skill that can be achieved with a little practice. In the course of reading, one should watch carefully to see whether the author bases his statements on substantial, cited information and evidence (this is a test required as much in reading a newspaper as in reading art history). Does the author give his conclusions, impressions, or judgments without any substantiating evidence or documentation? If he does, he is a dangerous source from which to draw ideas, even if his writing is exemplary. The difficulty in handling such impressionistic writing—writing that gives the author's views without providing the basis for them—is that there is no way of verifying it. In general, one must be wary of the writer on art who spins out long subjective theses without providing factual, documentary underpinning. A professional art historian has the responsibility not only for providing accurate conclusions, but also for providing the evidence upon which he bases his statements.

In the field of art, particularly, there are books and magazines that contain little more than the author's enthusiasm. Book counters and magazine stands are full of uncritical accounts of artists' lives that stress the romantic and exotic, the dramatic intensity of being an artist (in the popular, very misguided view). There are innumerable picture books, loaded with magnificent color illustrations, whose commentary is chatty, exciting, gossipy, evaluative, spiced with amusing anecdotes, but usually terribly inaccurate, based on third-hand information, which in the process of being made appealing has been badly mauled by the writer's biases. Historians rarely take notice of these casual publications, which find their way onto library shelves and assume a disguise of respectability by standing next to a responsible book on an artist or period.

Fictionalized accounts of artists' lives are, if well done, delightful to read and give a vivid picture of the time in which the artist lived. But one must remember that these are fiction based on fact, that the atmosphere they conjure up may be authentic, but that they are not intended for and should not be used as source books for further study.

Taking Notes. Almost any standard English composition book provides suggested formats for taking notes prior to writing a research paper. Any of the recommended systems, either in notebook or notecard form, can be adopted for art history research with minor modifications to take account of the specialized type of material.

The usual practices of keeping a bibliography of the literature read and of maintaining careful account of the page or pages from which specific information comes should be used, but, in addition, a careful record should be kept of the names and locations of art works referred to and where pertinent illustrations may be found.

Writing the Paper. Everyone has his own writing style. There is no formula to guarantee a "well written" paper, but there are some general practices which help protect writers from what most teachers would regard as poor productions. An essay is an attempt to communicate information and ideas to someone else. Thus, simplicity and clarity of writing, without sacrifice of content, are two of the most sought-after characteristics of writing. Dullness is not the necessary companion of simplicity and clarity; tortured, elaborate, highly idiosyncratic prose and format are not the necessary elements for interesting reading. Unsupported, sweeping generalizations do not demonstrate that the author knows what he is talking about; nor does the documenting of each successive sentence with a note guarantee "solid" research, if no clear thesis emerges.

Cursory examination of several professional writers of art history will show that their composition generally falls into three parts: 1) concise introductory statement of purpose, the nature of the problem to be discussed, the reason for studying this material; 2) introduction of the evidence and the examination, description, or discussion and interpretation of the data which form the main body of the paper; 3) summarizing statement that presents the conclusions that can be drawn from the previous discussion. This pattern is most useful in composing a paper, and while these three parts may be amplified and artfully worked together, the organization of the paper and the substance of what is being said should never be obscured by elaborate artifices of language or unnecessarily involved treatment.

Always write to the point. Keep in mind the specific problem or question that is the subject of the paper, and write on that and nothing else. If the problem under discussion is, for example, the narrative style in Giotto's frescoes, then do not go off tangentially into an abbreviated history of early Renaissance or late Medieval painting, or into an evaluation of nineteenth-century criticism of Giotto, or into an analysis of the chemical content of Giotto's paint, or into the anecdotes of Giotto's financial manipulations. These items may have some relevance to the topic at hand (Giotto's "narrative style"), but within the limited time and space of a research paper only material absolutely essential to the problem should remain; all else should be removed.

Plunge directly and immediately into the primary subject of the paper. As a general rule, avoid long introductions that both the writer and the reader must wade through before coming to the heart of the matter. An essay on the aims and ideas of the Bauhaus School need not begin with a history of design through the ages; a study of the Shingle style in American architecture does not need to be introduced by an account of architectural development in the United States. That paper on Giotto's narrative style need not be introduced by a summary of the condition of art at the beginning of the fourteenth century in Italy, or by a biography of the artist, or by a bird's-eye-view of the history of scholarship on Giotto. In reading on the Bauhaus, the Shingle style, or Giotto to prepare a paper, it is necessary to cover such material, and one needs to have digested it to write intelligently on his particular topic, but only a small part of what one reads and puts into one's notes should ever appear in a final essay. Research, like the iceberg, is only fractionally visible to the observer. The vast background of material absorbed contributes to the topic under consideration, but is not necessarily a part of the final scholarship produced. Many writers, after finishing the first draft of a paper, will go back and almost automatically discard the first few introductory paragraphs, or even pages, recognizing that they served their purpose in helping to organize and clarify the author's thoughts, but can now be discarded.

Double-check the first few sentences of the paper to be certain that they tell the reader what the paper will discuss; very clear definition of this point at the outset helps immeasureably in the subsequent writing. The first few sentences should make clear what aspect of research is being undertaken; a study, analysis, investigation, or evaluation of an artist, a style, a work of art, comparative works, comparative periods. A helpful motto to remember is that if you cannot clearly state for the reader in a few words the precise nature of the problem on which you are writing, then you probably have not clearly defined the topic for yourself. The first or second paragraph should also briefly locate the substance of the paper: what period? what style? what dates? what artist(s)?, what country? It would do no harm to follow the journalistic rule of getting into the first sentence of a story the five "Ws": who, what, when, where, why? One need not be that puritanical, nor ploddingly methodical, but one should not stray too far from such simple principles.

In the course of composing a paper, one should always ask the question, "How do I know this?" If the writer forces himself to document or justify each statement made, the report will be accurate and concise, with clear distinction among fact, interpretation of fact, hypotheses based on fact, guesses related to fact, and imagination at odds with fact. A good paper may contain all of these elements; it is only essential that the reader (*and* the writer) be absolutely clear which is which, lest he (and the writer) be misled into mistaking fancy for fact.

Students frequently ask to what extent their papers can be creative, that is, express their own ideas and conclusions. The answer depends to a great extent upon the ability and knowledge of the student in the area he is treating and the nature of that topic. Obviously, the student well acquainted with a field has the greater opportunity to bring his own insights and ideas into a paper than does the writer who is just beginning his study of the subject. Creative scholarship springs from profound knowledge, not innocence of a subject. But some research topics lend themselves naturally to a more creative, personal, or inventive approach than do others. A paper on the philosophical implications of DaDa or Funk art, for example, no doubt will be based on more suppositional ideas and personal evaluations than, say, an essay on the historical sources of these same movements. Art history is, after all, a historical discipline first and foremost, and history has to do with the theoretical reconstruction and interpretation of past events and monuments on the basis of surviving evidence. A historian must not evade or ignore evidence, and he cannot ask his reader to accept a point of view or a conclusion on the basis of faith alone.

Research papers should not be written for the specialist reader, but rather for that hypothetical average intelligent man. It is best to assume that the reader of the paper will have no prior knowledge of the intricacies of the matter under discussion. One must not take for granted that the reader will know what is meant without a clear and concise explanation, or that he will be familiar with data and objects which are referred to in passing without any identification. Abstruse, complex, and recondite writing that utilizes a maximum of technical jargon is a facile skill easily learned with a minimum of practice; it is also of little value. Much greater patience, adroitness, and artistry are required to write profound ideas in simple, easily understood terms.

There is no hard-and-fast rule as to how much information must be supplied in a paper, how much about any artist mentioned, any work of art discussed, any style referred to. One has to attempt to distinguish between what can be reasonably assumed to be common knowledge and uncommon knowledge on the part of the reader. Perhaps a few examples will illustrate the distinction. One can refer to the *Mona Lisa* without further identification (the "average" reader can be expected to know who painted it, that it is a painting, approximately when it was painted, and in what country its creator lived). However, reference to the "Mona Lisa" from Nimrud must carry some explanation (that it is a Syrian ivory found at the ancient Assyrian capital of Nimrud and so-named after the Leonardo painting because it, too, represents a lovely smiling female). And while one can safely assume that the reader has heard of the Mona Lisa Smile, and its author Leonardo da Vinci, one had best explain what is meant by the "veduta" landscape and identify the painter who is connected with it (Luca Carlevaris). More difficult to decide is whether one needs to offer explanation if the term "archaic smile" is used; will that average reader know the term as a commonplace in Greek art? The rule to follow is when in doubt, it is best to explain. Some technical terms of art history may be used without going into explanatory footnotes: Gothic period, Cubism, three-point perspective, fresco, peripteral, Baroque, Barbizonist. But the same is not true for less frequently used terms which should be explained: Minussinsk Period, Tachism, shifting point of reference, *opus sectile, distyle in antis,* daedelic, Kano artists. Once again, if the term is somewhat specialized and has not been met with frequently in reading, give the reader at least a parenthetical explanation.

Using Notes. Footnotes or notes placed in a separate section after the text frequently are troublesome to the student writer and a bore to the reader. The difficulty, however, does not lie in the institution of notes but rather in their misuse. Neither extreme—annotating every bit of information offered or eliminating all notes—is an equitable solution. In general, notes are useful as containers for necessary information that supports the text of the paper but is not part of the paper itself. While there are many types of notes, and many ways of using them, a simple plan for the beginner in research is to use notes to hold four types of material.

First, use footnotes or back notes to acknowledge the source of specific information that appears in the body of the paper. Here they serve as an honorable and courteous acknowledgment that the material quoted or cited or paraphrased originated with someone else and that the original author deserves the credit for the statement.

Second, use notes to direct the reader to sources where he can find fuller discussion of the material mentioned in passing in the body of the text.

Third, use notes to hold minor digressions or provide additional information which will help the reader to appreciate the matter under discussion in the text but which are not absolutely necessary to the text. That is, the note is used in the manner of an essential aside. Such an aside may take the form sometimes of contrary evidence to that presented in the body of the text or of conflicting opinion.

Fourth, use notes to contain documentation on works of art mentioned in the text, to give the dimensions, museum locations, owners, accession numbers.

There is no single style to be used in composing notes, although there are some traditional forms of ordering and abbreviation which can be found in any English composition handbook. Some schools advise the use of one particular style manual or another, but that is a matter of local preference. Hence, unless one is instructed to follow some specific form, a good rule of thumb is to use the footnote or back note format that will make the material contained in the note clear and easy to follow, that is, as brief as possible, and then to stick to that format without deviation. The note must contain: last name and first name or initials of the author, the exact title of the book or article as printed, the name of the journal (if the reference is to an article), the volume number (if any), the place of publication (for books, not for journals), the year of publication, the edition (if more than one), and the specific page(s) and/or illustration(s) to which the text refers.

Some note references may require more information than that listed above, and some less. For example, reference to a *Festschrift* (a volume of essays written by several people to honor a friend or teacher) or a symposium published in a single volume should also provide the name of the editor of the book, as well as the name of the author of the specific article and the title of the article, in addition to the title of the book. A newspaper reference will require the month, day, and year of publication. In contrast, a reference to a standard encyclopedia usually requires only the name of the encyclopedia, the edition, and the title of the article. A simple test for the adequacy and clarity of a note is for the student to go to the library and see if he can locate without undue time or difficulty the book or article mentioned in the note with only the information given there. If the author of the paper has trouble finding the source, so will the reader, and the note will not have served its purpose.

One of the questions most often asked by the student is to what extent must he document in a note the material on which he is writing. By its very nature a research paper is composed basically of information obtained elsewhere which leads the student to his own, unique contributions. Obviously, however, every sentence in a paper should not be footnoted. There is no rule of documentation beyond reasonableness. A direct quotation of someone else's words requires a note. Paraphrasing specific information requires the same courtesy. But information which has general currency in the field, which can be found in most any writing on the subject, need not be documented. To give obvious examples of statements that need not be cited in a note: that Phidias was a Greek sculptor of the fifth century B.C. in Athens and a friend of Pericles; that Chartres cathedral is a Catholic Medieval monument in France whose earliest part is that forming the west portal; that Picasso's painting of the *Demoiselles d'Avignon* is often regarded as the first Cubist painting. (Any of these statements *may* contain an error, but they represent commonly held and often documented positions.) However, specialized data, information which is subject to disagreement, and material to be found only after a good deal of searching, usually needs to be documented. For example, one would provide authority for stating the following: that Phidias worked on the statue of Athena Parthenos prior to that of Zeus of Olympia (there is some question as to which came first); that the exact year of the beginning of the building of the west portal at Chartres was such and such (precise dating of medieval monuments is usually difficult); that Picasso's *Demoiselles d'Avignon* was inspired by Cézanne's bathers series (has this been proven, or is it a speculation?).

There is no value in referring in a note to material not consulted by the writer of the paper. And there is almost as little use in providing a note that refers the reader to a whole book or a large section of material (such as: "See pages 9–327"). The most useful citation is one which sends the reader to the specific page or two on which the information is to be found. Of course, there are exceptions, times when an author might want to inform a reader that a particular book covering a given subject has, indeed, been written, but these are definitely exceptions and not the rule.

A paper with carefully composed notes usually does not require a bibliography. The bibliography (the sources from which the author of the paper worked) will be documented in the notes; to put all of the references at the end of the paper is a duplication. However, it is sometimes convenient to have all pertinent references, materials consulted, compiled in one place as a bibliography. A bibliography, like notes, must contain all the information that will facilitate the locating of materials. Generally, bibliographies are arranged in alphabetical order by author, but, depending upon the length and complexity of the paper, other arrangements might be more useful. For example, books and journal articles may be listed separately; or, the variously published writings of an artist may be separated from the consulted source material about the artist; or the references consulted on several artists may be arranged alphabetically by artist. Some authors have a tendency to proliferate notes and bibliographical entries, as if to make absolutely clear to the reader that they have left no stone unturned in their study; other writers will provide only two or three cryptic entries. Overuse of notes and bibliographical citations is a burden to the writer and a nuisance to the reader; underuse diminishes the authority of the writing and eliminates a valuable aid for the reader.

To Quote or Not to Quote? Student authors are often guilty of unintentional plagiarism—copying the exact language or ideas of someone else without acknowledging that the writing is not their own. Or, sometimes, to avoid technical plagiarism, the writer may change a word or sentence here and there, or put together two sentences from two different sources. Such practices should be avoided, first, because of the legal and moral implications of passing off as one's own words or ideas those which belong to someone else. But, second, and perhaps more important, is that in copying or reorganizing another's work, the student bypasses one of the most important learning experiences that writing research papers provides: taking the thoughts of others, digesting them, integrating them with one's own ideas, and then expressing oneself clearly and accurately in one's own language. No one learns how to think and write by rephrasing and copying another's thoughts and language.

Many students feel, often quite erroneously, that the published writing they read is written in the best of all possible forms; why should the student attempt to recast and rewrite what he has read in his less skilled, less informed style? Regardless of the merit of the published text, it should be remembered that one learns more about art history and how to write art history when material is read, thoroughly digested, and then recomposed in one's own terms. The process of rephrasing and synthesizing what others have written forces the writer to understand the material fully. The student should also remember that while he may not have the practiced pen and style of the experienced writer, his own writing may have a freshness, clarity, and simplicity of expression that the professional writer has lost. Student writing often contains a fresh, clear, uncluttered enthusiasm or point of view which is refreshing to read.

Extensive quotations are dull to copy and dull to read. In general, they should be avoided. It is almost always better to summarize and synthesize than to quote at length. There are times when the precise phrasing of a source is necessary, and the phrase or sentence(s) should be quoted, particularly when the artist himself is writing about his work. However, the more interesting paper usually is one which provides the greatest opportunity for learning, that product which is most completely the work of the student author.

Usually students err on the side of relying too heavily upon quoted statements. Quotations are essential only when the precise phrasing of the source is essential to the understanding of the subject under discussion. Thus, it is not necessary to quote an author's summary biography of Michelangelo, but one may want to quote the exact wording of Michelangelo's near contemporary Vasari when he states a "fact" about the sculptor's life over which there is some serious question or about which we have no other source of information. Most quotations in art history research deal with information that comes from a primary source (such as Vasari's *Lives* or Vincent van Gogh's letters).

Extensive use of quotations gives an essay not so much the feel of authority as of pretentiousness and artificiality. Some types of research require more extensive use of quotations than others. For example, a study of Vincent van Gogh's ideas about painting, about how he approached his subject matter and what he found most vital in the process of setting down his compositions, would find most forceful expression in direct transcriptions of the painter's words, the sense of which might be unintentionally altered in a rephrasing. But the opposite is true in, say, a study of the character of the sculptural program on the cathedral at Chartres; it would be uselessly encumbered by fulsome quotations from the thousands of analyses that have been written by students of Medieval art. Probably the best material to quote in art history is the work of art itself; the commentaries on the work of art are always of secondary importance and are necessarily interpretative and subjective views.

Referring to Works of Art. Whenever an art object or monument is mentioned, the author should provide as complete identifying information as possible. A reference to "Bellini's Madonna" is useless (which Madonna painting by which Bellini?). The ideal citation, usually placed in a footnote so as not to interrupt the text with technical details, will give the full name of the artist, the title of the work, the date assigned to it, the material or technique (oil on canvas, fresco, bronze, lithography, mixed media), the present location of the work, and its dimensions:

Paul Cézanne, *Mt. S. Victoire from Bibemus Quarry*. circa 1898. Oil on canvas. Baltimore Museum of Art. 25-1/2″ × 32″.

Some works, of course, will not need such ample documentation. Michelangelo need not be referred to by his full name; the cathedral at Chartres need not have its material or technique cited; the dimensions of a manuscript miniature probably will not be essential; citing the location of the Louvre is unnecessary.

The more illustrations a paper carries, the better it is, but it is usually not feasible to illustrate every work of art referred to in an essay. Those works mentioned but not illustrated should be accompanied by a note telling the reader where he may see the object or an illustration of it. For the cathedral at Chartres (which is illustrated abundantly) such a note is not necessary, but the referral for Cézanne's painting in the Baltimore Museum of Art is most helpful ("For illustration, see, D. G. Cleaver, *Art, An Introduction*. New York, 1966, pl. 83.").

An illustration included in a paper should carry all the information mentioned above *and* the source of the photograph, reproduction, or drawing.

Photo: Detroit Institute of Arts.
Photo after: Cleaver, *Art,* pl. 83.
Illustration: University prints.
Drawing after: Cleaver, *Art,* pl. 83.

Foreign Language Quotations. Unfortunately for the English-reading student, much of the writing of concern to the art historian is in a foreign language. Courtesy demands that, whenever possible, material in a foreign language be translated for the reader. The writer should assume that his reader will know no other language than the one in which his paper is written. Peppering an essay with foreign phrases and quotations is pretentious rather than professional. Sometimes, however, the particular quality of the quotation in its original language is deemed important, when the precise meaning or shades of meaning can only be grasped fully in the exact words of the author. Then the foreign phrase should be given, but the author should also append his translation in a note. Some phrases are encountered in reading for which an exact English equivalent is elusive (words like *Gemütlichkeit* or *Kunstwollen*), but even then an approximate translation along with the foreign term is preferable to none at all. Some foreign words and phrases are so standard in talking and writing on art history that they can be used without further explanation (such as Sfumato, chiaroscuro, chevet, repoussoir, fresco secco). But again, when in doubt, translate.

Titles of books need not be translated, although it is helpful to append a translation if they appear in a script other than Latin or in a language fairly unfamiliar to the Western eye. Thus, a Japanese title should be written in Latin characters to be followed by a translation in parentheses.

There is no firm agreement on how to give names of art objects. Picasso's *Demoiselles d'Avignon* appears to be so well known by that name that one rarely if ever meets the painting with the English title *Young Ladies of Avignon*. The Church of the *Holy Wisdom* in Istanbul is sometimes so labeled, but is more commonly referred to as the *Hagia Sophia* or the *Sancta Sophia*. Usually the great works of art of the past carry a general descriptive designation rather than a unique title given by the artist (descriptive titles such as the Baptism of Christ, the Finding of Moses, Madonna and Child, the Death of Socrates, Study of a Nude), and these should be given in English. However, the descriptive title *Pietà* is usually so given and not translated into English. Statues of archaic Greek male youths are sometimes so labeled, but the term *Kouroi* is commonly used. Manet's *Déjeuner sur l'herbe* is so familiar by its French title that to use its English equivalent sounds a bit stilted, but it would be pompous to refer to his *Execution of Maximilian* in French.

A Final Checklist for the Research Paper. Most writers bring their papers through a series of rough drafts, and rare indeed is the writer whose first draft of a paper is ready for the typist. Listed here are some checkpoints that may be useful in judging the adequacy of a draft.

1. Is the topic stated precisely and clearly at the beginning of the paper?

2. Has the opening paragraph given the who, what, when, and where of the topic under discussion?

3. Have specific works of arts and artists been cited to document statements?

4. Has each work of art and monument been documented as to artist, material, location, date, etc.?

5. Has the temptation to include material that is interesting but not essential to the paper been resisted?

6. Have background materials, biographical commonplaces, over-extended quotations of what other authors have had to say, and generalized historical summaries of great stretches of time been reduced to an absolute minimum or eliminated?

7. Has the paper concentrated only on the most important aspects of the topic and not gone off on tangents that are useful only in a much longer, more comprehensive study?

8. Has the paper been closed with a succinct recapitulation of the major points and conclusions reached through the study?

9. Have the footnotes been kept to a minimum but adequate level, and do they follow a clear and consistent format?

10. Has the paper been proofread in its final stage for mispellings, typographical errors, substandard English, and omissions?

The student of art history should be, above all students, most concerned with the visual appearance of his paper. His interest is in the visual arts. While neatness of appearance and care in presentation may not enhance the substantive quality of the paper, they will make for more enjoyable reading. The reader of an art history paper is trained to respond to visual appearances; he should not be disappointed at his first impression of the newly created work.

LIBRARY, MUSEUM, AND ART HISTORY LITERATURE

Although American college and public libraries follow similar patterns of organization and operation, no two libraries are identical. Hence, these general remarks, are broadly applicable but may need modification in any particular situation when the student goes to the library to work on an art history problem.

Only the completely uninitiated student is surprised to find that his college or public library does not have one or several books and journals that he is seeking. All libraries have their strengths and weaknesses, although the art history shortcomings of such excellent libraries as the New York Public Library or the Library of the Metropolitan Museum of Art may not be as easily found as those of more modest institutions. The size of the art history collection of any library depends to a large extent on the age of the library, its location, its financial resources, its functions and obligations in the community that supports it, the interests and tastes of the librarians who have successively staffed it, and its general operating policies. Obviously, a local public branch library whose primary concern is to provide literature for the general community will not have the art history book resources that can be found in a university or art museum library. A new college, or one with a recently established art history program, will not have as extensive and comprehensive a collection as the library of an institution with a long-established curriculum of art history.

It is axiomatic that the richer the library resources he has, the easier the student's task of research. But no matter how great and famous a library, it will not have on its shelves all the art history literature ever published. Professional art historians rarely limit themselves to one or two libraries, but rather avail themselves of the resources of many through the medium of interlibrary loans, microfilms, and visits to distant libraries. Thus, while it is disappointing not to find a desired book in the nearest library, a wholesale condemnation of that library is hardly in order. While the student cannot afford extensive travel to find books, he can frequently have access not only to the campus library, but also to local public and museum libraries. In addition, his college library probably has a system for obtaining books via interlibrary loans, a central library pool, and microfilms, or may be able to obtain short works (such as journal articles) by any of several reproduction techniques.

All the books and journals listed in this handbook may not be available locally, although they have been selected because they are the standard, easily obtainable reference tools. Whenever possible, more than one reference book of any kind has been included in the list to help overcome the problem of unavailability. However, the reader will be agreeably surprised to find how many of these works are on the shelves of small community libraries as well as in the colleges.

First Step in Research: Locating Library Materials. Libraries hold many kinds of "published" materials other than books and journals, such as microfilm, microcards, clippings, newspapers, pamphlets, reports, documents, picture files, manuscripts, dissertations, maps, and charts. Everything held by a library (with some exceptions which will hardly affect the student beginning research) is listed in the library's card catalog, which is an index to its holdings. Hence, the place to begin in a library is at that catalog.

Libraries catalog their holdings by author, subject, and title, as well as, for example, by sponsoring institution, region, country, agency, or institute, when appropriate. Articles published in journals or collections, that is, writings that are part of a volume containing materials by several hands, are not listed in the general library catalog unless the article is published or bound separately. Articles contained in larger works are to be located in the several types of indices mentioned in this handbook.

The catalog card for a book contains helpful information that may be utilized before obtaining the book itself: the facts of publication (place, publishing house, date) the number of volumes, the number of the edition, the number of copies held by the library, the size of the book, whether it is illustrated, and often the birth and death dates of the author and a brief summary of the book's contents. But most important is the numerical designation, the catalog number assigned to the book in that library and the means by which it can be located on the shelves.

Two numerical systems are generally used in the United States—Dewey Decimal and the Library of Congress—with local adaptations made by different libraries. In terms of locating the book in the library, it matters little which system is used. The student must only be certain that when he leaves the catalog file to find his book he is armed with the *complete* numerical designation for the specific item, including volume and edition, that he wants to locate. That call number or shelf number is made up of a combination of letters and digits, but it also may include the date of the edition, a series number, or a volume number. All of these data are necessary to locate the desired book.

Journals and magazines are filed in different manners in different libraries. Sometimes they carry no numerical designation, but rather are arranged alphabetically by title on the shelves; in some libraries they carry a shelf number and are placed in the stacks along with books on the same subject.

Some libraries permit the student to go into the stacks to retrieve his books; others permit only the library staff to get books upon presentation of the catalog number. Most libraries have a combination of open and closed stacks. No matter what system a library uses, there are two important points to remember: 1) it is a waste of time and usually fruitless to go to the book shelves to locate a book without first consulting the card catalog and obtaining the book's numerical designation; 2) it must never be assumed that a book not on the shelf, where its number indicates it should be, must therefore be withdrawn and not available. Ask the librarian for aid.

Books are arranged in libraries according to categories. A librarian may have a general idea where a specific book is shelved according to the type of subject matter it contains, but even he would want the numerical designation from the card catalog to help him locate it. Many books, particularly art books (because they often are published in large sizes and have expensive illustrations), are placed in a special location for a variety of reasons: books with a large format may be placed on special oversized shelves or folio shelves; rare or unusually expensive books, or elaborately illustrated books, may be kept in special security areas; very old or infrequently used books may be placed in storage facilities; books currently used by a particular course in art history may be placed on special reserve shelves; books used mainly for reference may be shelved in a special reference area. Given this range of possibilities, it is accepted practice in library work to consult, first, the general card catalog to ascertain that the library has the book and where it is located, and then, if the material listed cannot be located on the shelf, to consult the librarian. Librarians are specialists in locating books, and they have access to a "shelf list" that tells where the book is located in the library. They can quickly determine where the book is, and, in addition, they are extremely helpful in suggesting alternate, and frequently more useful books and sources than those being sought which are unavailable (in circulation, in the bindery, misplaced, or stolen).

Second Step in Research: Obtaining a Reading List. Every art history topic has its own particular requirements which dictate to a large extent how one should proceed in gathering and organizing library resources. A few guidelines can be sketched which, if not too practical in some instances of advanced study, can serve the student as a point of departure for developing his own system of retrieving information in a research project.

Usually a student has a headstart on a list of books to be consulted for his research topic in the form of the reading list supplied by his course instructor. A classroom bibliography may be broad, but the notes and bibliographies contained in the listed books will offer entrance into the highly specialized literature that is basic to all serious research. This manner of proceeding is quite common in research work: follow the source material noted by one author and then note the sources mentioned in each work to which the first has referred, and so on. This technique has three advantages: 1) it quickly permits the building of an extensive bibliography; 2) it leads even the most uninitiated beginner in a special area back to the basic source material; and 3) it rapidly familiarizes the student with the names of the important contributors in the field, those whose books are most often referred to, and, by the fact of their absence in bibliographies and footnotes, warns students away from authors who have no professional standing in the subject.

If one does not have the advantage of a readymade reading list, materials on the subject under study can quickly be found in the various bibliographical guides, indices, and encyclopedias whose notes and suggestions for additional reading will refer one to more specialized studies. The library card catalog can be very helpful once again, this time in providing the basis of a bibliography under its subject headings. For example, to find the kinds of reading materials that would assist the researcher in a study of some aspect of Michelangelo, in the library one should first check the general card catalog under such listings as: Michelangelo; Art—Italian; Art—Renaissance; Architecture—Italian; Architecture—Renaissance; Sculpture. And one should not ignore possible related headings, such as Renaissance, Rome, de Medicis, etc.

After compiling the list of books that may be useful in the research project, the next step should be a perusal of the periodical literature, articles that have appeared in journals, magazines, museum bulletins, and catalogs. The *Art Index* (B-17) provides an excellent, if not complete, listing, year by year, of articles that have appeared in a broad selection of journals and museum bulletins. With references from the *Art Index* added to sources obtained from the card catalog, the student will have gained a prospective list of source materials with which to begin his reading, while he continues to compile further possible references.

Some of the books and articles, once they have been briefly examined, will be quickly discovered to be not directly on the topic and discarded, while some others may only duplicate information gained elsewhere. Some materials will be found to be flimsy or just a repetition of popularly produced information. This culling of sources is sometimes discouraging, but certainly not a waste of time. A large part of any research project is involved in evaluating information, discarding the useless, following leads that result in deadends, and finding out what is *not* contained in the literature consulted. Only a small part of one's total searching and reading appears in the finished product, the research paper.

In the course of preparing a paper on, say, some aspect of Michelangelo's painting or sculpture, many references will be made by authors one consults that are not explained—references to certain Italian noble families, to technical matters of stone carving or fresco painting, to Biblical subjects or mythological stories. It is at these points in reading that the encyclopedias and dictionaries, biographical handbooks, and lexicons are most valuable to find quickly and easily the location, say, of the Carrara quarries, the vital statistics on Lorenzo di Medici, the identification of the Sibyls, the origin of the term Mannerist, the size of the Sistine Chapel, the scope of Papal power in Renaissance Italy, the iconography of the Last Judgment, the trustworthiness of Vasari. The more specialized a research project is, the more sophisticated the techniques required, but once the fairly simple procedure for locating basic information has become a matter of course, the road to more recondite and exacting studies is open.

Locating Books and Periodicals. Everyone experiences occasional difficulty finding some book or journal. Sometimes it is the loss of the author's name or the title of the book that causes the trouble; sometimes a periodical cannot be found because its precise name is not known, or it is difficult to find how it is listed in the library. The shelving of periodical literature is usually the greatest mystery to the non-librarian who is at a loss to know where to find, for example, the listing for the (fictional) *P*roceedings of the *S*ixth *A*nnual *W*orld *C*ongress of the *I*nternational *A*rt Historical *S*ociety held in the *S*iena Fine Arts Seminary which sponsored the conference and published it.

The librarian should, of course, be consulted when such problems arise, but there are also some quick references one can consult in addition. For example, if one is not sure that a book exists, or if the name is correct as it appears in some casual notes, a check of the holdings of one of the large libraries can usually verify the book. Thus, a book title that cannot be located in the library catalog can be sought in the catalogs of the Library of Congress, or the British Museum, or the Metropolitan Museum of Art. The multi-volume Library of Congress catalog is in all college libraries. Many will have those of the British Museum and the Metropolitan Museum, and an examination of the references located on the adjacent shelves will probably also reveal catalogs of other major libraries in this country and abroad. While no library has a listing for every piece of literature ever published, unless the item sought is quite exotic, the chances are very good that the object of one's search will appear in one of the three catalogs mentioned here. If the book appears in the catalog of the major library but not in one's local library, then assistance should be obtained from the librarian to determine if it is possible to get the book locally by some type of loan or reproduction procedure.

To find the exact name of a periodical, or how it is listed, one can consult the several bound volumes that comprise the *Union List of Serials* (available in all libraries) which not only tells how the volumes are shelved in the library, but also lists which libraries hold the periodical.

Finally, when one exhausts his own resources and still is left with some question marks in his bibliography, he should consult the librarian. A good librarian can perform miracles, locating materials on impossibly slender clues. Following a librarian as he goes about locating a particuarly mischievous title or spectral author provides a lesson in search procedure that no library handbook can duplicate.

Types of Art History Books. The amount and variety of art works forming the substance of art history are staggering—the works of all peoples of all times—and such a compilation can never be encompassed in any one book or set of books. No matter how broad the scope of any set of volumes on the history of art, only a selected portion of the accumulated works left by the past, and the knowledge we have about them can be presented (which is one major reason why the art historian is also a critic in that he must constantly select which works and artists are important to history and which may be left undisturbed). Thus, all authors exercise their selective faculties in deciding what to present to the reader, and no book should be considered as if it were the final and definitive work (as publishers' advertisements will modestly state); no book should be criticized because it is not absolutely comprehensive.

What an art historian finally includes in his book and what he decides to omit depend to a large extent upon the book's intended use and audience. Hence, although the study of art history is a relatively recent scholarly development (compared to that of astronomy, philosophy, mathematics, and general history), a bewildering variety of literature on the arts has accumulated to satisfy many different appetites. The bibliographical section of this handbook lists various references and survey works with suggestions for their use. The books provide different categories of information. The general history books of periods and nations provide the broad panoramic studies, and the specialized studies and monographs focus on smaller segments of the art history landscape. Such studies range from intensive examinations of a period or a style (Gallo-Roman sculpture of France, Sung painting, Cubism) to analyses of single works or monuments (see, for example, Bieber's study of the *Laocoon,* Arnheim's recapitulation of the genesis of the *Guernica* by Picasso, or Wormald's study of the *Utrecht Psalter*). Less than book-length studies, pamphlets and bulletin and journal articles usually tackle a single problem, such as the identification of the author of a painting, the confirmation of the exact date of an artist's last work, or the authenticating of an antiquity. Monographs devoted to a single artist and his production range from short appreciations of an artist's work and contribution, to full-length studies of the man's life and a cataloging of his accomplishments in several volumes.

After using the basic survey books, the student likely will read extensively in this type of bibliographical material, basing his research on the information found there. From there he proceeds to the primary documents mentioned previously, the mass of written works contemporary with the art under study. To understand the painting of Vincent van Gogh, one must read his letters to his family and friends. No true estimate of the genius of Leonardo da Vinci can be made without reading his notebooks. Any estimate of the part played by Edouard Manet in the development of Realism must be partly based on the essays of his friend Émile Zola. No study of the great Persian monument at Persepolis can be undertaken without a close reading of Herodotus. The aims of the Italian Surrealists are carefully spelled out in their manifestos. Writings by historically important personalities—such as the several mentioned above—are easily obtained in English translations at most moderate-sized libraries.

More difficult to locate, and frequently unavailable except in the original language, are documents of less known artists and the many documents that accumulate in an artist's day to day living which can have important bearings upon the study of his work. Legal documents (birth, marriage, death, admission to guilds) and contracts (between artist and patron or master and apprentice), as well as records of sales, commissions, and travels may be found in some libraries, but more often the art history student must travel to city halls, archives, and sundry repositories to locate such material, unless it has been previously studied and incorporated into a biography. The studies of the advanced student of art history must utilize this kind of primary documentation.

It is important to differentiate between biographies of artists and the historical fiction books about the arts and artists. Too much stress cannot be placed upon distinguishing between the two types of literature. The romantic aura that so often surrounds the arts and artists in popular imagination has promoted the writing of stories of lives of artists that are more or less drawn from the known data. A factual, documented account of the career of an artist is one thing, but a story of romantic adventure that for the sake of drama and excitement distorts, creates, and dismisses some facts in the manufacture of a fabric woven from sense and nonsense is quite another matter. Many authors are honest in their intent, stating at the very onset of their "biography" that they are writing a fictionalized account based on the life of the artist, but too often the unwary reader has no prior indication that what he is reading is creative writing and not accurate biography.

All biographers must reconstruct to a certain degree, but then only to the degree that the known facts will support the reconstruction and will not be distorted by the suppositions. The storytelling biographer goes beyond what the known facts will permit, allowing his imagination to reconstitute large areas of the artist's life without sufficient basis, and then arbitrarily interpreting some factual details out of context to lend an air of authenticity to the imaginative tale. Unfortunately there is no clear dividing line between authentic and fictionalized biography; rather, the distinction is one of degree. The experienced reader of artist's biography usually can sense the difference in only a few pages of writing—perhaps in the manner of writing, the way in which words are used, the manner in which some aspects are glossed over while others are overdrawn, the degree to which the author can penetrate with absolute certainty into the innermost thoughts of the artist. In general, the carefully prepared, factually based biography will carry some type of notes or appendix wherein the author lists and/or discusses the sources of his information, documents, interviews, letters, and diaries.

This repeated warning against fictionalized biographies of artists (of which the crudest appear as motion picture and television productions) is not intended as a condemnation of such books. They should be judged on their literary merit rather than on their authenticity; they should be read as fiction and not as history. The same is true, of course, of fictionalized accounts of historical periods or artistic episodes (a romance of the Middle Ages or the recounting of the artist life as lived in Montmartre). Well written historical novels can happily recreate an atmosphere of bygone times with a greater sense of actuality than can, perhaps, a dozen scholarly tomes. But in reading them one must never forget that he is holding a novel in his hands.

A similar problem exists in evaluating the historical worthiness of articles in magazines. Some of the most important research and writing in art history, as in any field of study, first appears in magazine and journal form. But matters having to do with art and artists are subject to broad magazine popularization. Most magazines in the United States will have sometime during the year an article or so dealing with artists or art. And, in addition, there are many magazines designed to popularize the arts. Usually the primary intent of such articles and magazines is to create an attractive essay that will hold the interest of the general reader for a short period and stimulate his enthusiasm for the subject. Such essays are not intended to be used as resource material for the art history student. Some very popular articles on art are written by authoritative pens and have substantial contents that can be extremely useful, but such writings are very rare, forcing the student to be chary of any and all such writing as a basis for study.

How does one distinguish between popular magazine articles based on enthusiasm rather than solid content? There are a few tests, although none is a foolproof guide. The general caliber of the magazine or journal in which the article appears is one index. A publication whose stock-in-trade is fashions, world news, politics, homemaking, travel, or adventure (or any combination thereof) will probably be of no use for art history purposes. Also, the reputation of the writer as a serious art historian is important. The quality and manner of exposition should be examined. (Warning: authoritative writing is not necessarily dull, and journalistic nonsense is not necessarily exciting to read.) There are some magazines which, while pompously declaring their dedication to the arts, are little more than arty; these can usually be immediately recognized by their use of expensive, lurid format that screams for attention.

Book shelves are laden with large-sized, thin, lavishly produced books of illustrations, picture books on art, that carry short introductions and appreciations. These books provide reproductions of works which the reader does not have the opportunity of seeing directly whenever he desires. Hence, the value of a picture book depends upon the excellence and faithfulness of the quality of the reproductions it contains. Modern photographic and printing techniques produce some remarkable picture books. The reproductions are often of such clarity, brilliance, and sharpness of detail that the original work looks a bit dingy in comparison with its photograph. No reproduction, no matter how carefully prepared (see R-203 for the technical problems involved), can be exactly faithful to or take the place of the original, but modern production techniques permit the student to come into contact, albeit secondhand, with works of art in all corners of the world.

The student using picture books should be on guard against the texts which accompany the illustrations; they are uneven in quality and of doubtful value to serious study. Usually the texts are kept to a minimum of words because the reason for the book's being is the illustrations. These introductory remarks may be succinct commentary on the art objects illustrated, or, less happily, a sentimental dab that tells little beyond the author's emotional state of being, a type of commentary that is all too common.

Sensitivity in evaluating the merits of published literature in the arts comes with experience in the daily reading of the many types. Critical standards and procedures of research are acquired slowly, almost unconsciously. As the student gains experience in using the library, he will find that he can not only more speedily retrieve material but also read only that literature most useful to him.

Using Book Reviews. Published reviews of art history books can be of practical value to the student by providing him with an estimate of the quality of a book and of the dependability of the book as a reference tool. Reviews of books are indexed in the *Art Index.* Book reviews also:

1. keep the student up to date on what is being published;
2. usually provide a synopsis of the contents of a book which helps the reader decide if he wants to look it up;
3. provide an additional insight, that of the reviewer, into the topic of the book;
4. frequently provide suggestions on related books;
5. may correct errors in the book or bring its contents up to date;
6. provide the critical estimate of at least one man as to the overall quality of the book and its value to the field of art history studies.

Reviews must be used with a degree of caution, however, and the reader must remember that he is reading the evaluation of another scholar whose writing also needs to be read critically. Perhaps the student can gain insight into using and judging reviews from the following brief outline of how book reviews come about.

First, the quality and character of a review will vary with the quality of the journal or paper in which it appears. Obviously, a review in a local newspaper will be at a different level than one published in a journal devoted to art history. The newspaper review may be well intentioned and provide a short summary of the book's contents, but though usually written by the general book reviewer for the paper, it may also have been written by the night editor's daughter whose total acquaintance with the field of art is at the hobby level. But even disregarding this type of popular reviewing and considering only that which appears in the professional literature of the arts and art history, one must still exercise caution in reading reviews.

Few journals publish unsolicited reviews. The standard practice is for publishers to send books to the journal in the hope of their being reviewed. For the publishers, reviews are primarily a means of advertising their books among the people most likely to purchase them. The journal uses reviews as a way of keeping its readership current on what is being published with a scholarly estimate of the worth of the new material. Books are usually assigned for review by the journal to scholars with special interests in the subject. The reviewer may be provided with a word limit and a deadline, but beyond that he is free to write his critical estimate without any restraint beyond that of his professional conscience.

What the reviewer chooses to write varies beyond description. Some reviews are straightforward summaries of the contents of the book; some reviews are critical studies of the material, frequently offering new evidence, alternate ideas, reinterpretations, corrections of fact, etc. Too many reviews are one-sided debates with the book's author (the author has no opportunity for immediate rebuttal). And, unfortunately, some reviews are highly personal, detailing what the reviewer would have written had he written the book (which of course he has not), and the review may be tinged with a personal animosity that springs from an old wound. Some reviews are tediously concerned with detailing of typographical errors; some are spleenitic, written on the assumption that a review is well done only if it fries the author. Some reviews are also the responses of friendship, loaded with laudatory phrases. The best reviews are written under the constraint that they are a mode of professional interchange of ideas, a responsibility that the historian owes to his discipline; the dullest reviews are written as a tedious chore for the payment of the free copy of the book being reviewed. The perfect review for student use provides a summary of the contents of the book, discussion of its most important aspects (in the reviewer's opinion), a summary of the best features and the shortcomings (again clearly stated as in the reviewer's opinion), and an expansion on some critical aspect of the volume on which the reviewer is particularly or perhaps uniquely qualified to comment. At the very least, reviews in professional journals will guide the student away from the ever-increasing volume of flimsy literature and help him to concentrate on the substantial writings.

Museum Research. Art collections are the laboratories for art history research. Both public and private museums as a rule are most helpful to the serious student, as well as open to the casual visitor. Museums are organized in various fashions, depending upon their size and financial resources. The museum has a curatorial staff—the people responsible for the acquisition, conservation, exhibition, and study of works of art—and also (depending upon size) staffs of educators, restorers, registrars, and librarians.

A large museum will divide the responsibility for its collections among several curators—one for Renaissance art, another for, say, American art, perhaps one for the ancient section, and so on. In small museums one or two curators may have to be responsible for all the works held, regardless of period or culture. Serious historical questions about any art work held by a museum should be addressed to the curator in charge (see listings under Museum Directories). Every collection has a registrar, the person responsible for the file information on every work held. Questions about the vital statistics of a work may be addressed to him. Museums both in the United States and abroad usually are very courteous in answering written queries.

Some museums have reference libraries, which may be open to serious students, and they may have extensive picture files and clipping files.

For a variety of reasons, not the least of which is security, museums regulate to different degrees the freedom of visitors in their galleries. Should the student wish to photograph, sketch, or measure objects in a museum, he should first obtain the museum's permission. Some museums freely give the required permission, while others may have strict rules governing the reproduction of works of art in any form. A museum may permit a visitor to photograph works in the permanent collection, but not works on temporary display which do not belong to the institute. Cameras may be permitted, but not tripods or flash bulbs; or such restrictions may be lifted if there are no crowds.

Curators generally are pleased to have students become seriously involved in the study of their holdings and will generously extend themselves in providing assistance. (A single experience of an unfriendly curator or librarian should be disregarded; he is the exception to the rule.)

Several museums in the United States have student curator programs, usually sponsored in conjunction with a local university. The student receives his formal art historical training at the university and then engages in on-the-job training, an internship, at the museum.

Museum Bulletins. A valuable source of information on works of art held by art institutes, museums, and galleries can be found in the bulletins published by these collectors. All large museums and many small ones publish pamphlet-sized bulletins annually, quarterly, or bimonthly which report on the activities of the museum and on the works of art acquired. The articles are usually short, written by the curatorial staff or specialists, and contain at least the basic documentation on the work of art. Some college libraries may subscribe to the bulletins of the very largest museums in the world, but only specialized art history reference libraries (such as those in art institutes) maintain fairly comprehensive holdings of large and small museum bulletins. Even though the student may not have ready access to a desired museum bulletin, he can easily obtain one; individual issues are inexpensive, and a letter to a museum will usually produce a copy for a small fee.

Museums publish in their bulletins their major accessions, many of their minor holdings, but, of course, not everything they have in their cabinets, on their walls, or in their vaults. Most museum bulletins will publish once a year a list of acquisitions in the past twelve months. The bulletin articles are not only good reference material for the studies they contain, but they also provide the primary documentation on works: dimensions, previous owners, bibliography, condition of the object, when and where it was exhibited previously. Thus, any study made on a work held by a museum will profit by consultation of the museum's bulletin.

Museums like to publish important works they have acquired as soon as possible after the accession. Hence, to locate a bulletin article on a work, one should first look into the bulletins issued the year of acquisition or the issues immediately following. The museum's registrar could quickly answer a query as to whether and where the object in question had been published.

Exhibition Catalogs. Almost all public exhibitions of art have some type of catalog published for the event. These catalogs vary in comprehensiveness from a simple listing of the titles of works to a fully annotated, book-length study of the object on exhibition. The catalog will provide the basic statistics on the objects, and thus will be extremely valuable to research and study. Some, if not all, the objects exhibited may be illustrated in the catalog, and the catalog may be the only place that some of these objects have ever been published. Also, the catalogs are most useful because the exhibition may hold works from private collections that have never had another public audience.

Unfortunately, it is very difficult to locate and maintain up-to-date records on exhibition catalogs. While no library holds a complete collection of exhibition catalogs, the advanced art history student will find that, should he want to consult a catalog extensively, he may be able to purchase a copy from the museum or gallery which sponsored the show. However, these catalogs usually are printed in limited numbers and are quickly sold out. Thus, there are serious drawbacks in attempting to consult exhibition catalogs, but they are very important in methodical research and well worth the effort of locating them.

Cataloging Art Works. Short papers in art history usually discuss a small handful of works of art, and the student does not need to devise an apparatus to keep them in order with their vital statistics. In contrast, a long paper that deals with perhaps dozens of works by a painter or many objects by different hands scattered about the world may require a simple cataloging procedure. One of the chief tools used in art history research is a running catalog of objects with which the student is dealing. The catalog provides a handy means of referring back to art works, of establishing the sequence of one work to another, of locating where a work is to be seen, is illustrated, or is discussed.

Keeping a catalog on large index cards during research on a long paper will prove to be well worth the time. All one need do is establish the format for the card and then, every time in reading a work is referred to, immediately complete a card and insert it into the file in its proper chronological position; when another discussion of a work for which a card had been previously made is encountered, then the card, located by the date of the object, can be taken out of the file and the new information added. A catalog file that contains the works of different artists would be ordered alphabetically by artist and then chronologically within each artist's category. Following is a list of suggested information that a catalog card may contain:

Name of artist

Title of work — Date of Work (absolute or approximate)

Medium (oil on canvas, marble, etching, terracotta, etc.)

Dimensions

Whether artist's signature and/or date appears on the work and, if so, how signed

Owner (name of collection, where located, accession number)

Bibliography (where published and illustrated)

Brief descriptive notes

At a more involved level of research, the advanced student may want to include: chronological list of previous owners of the work; chronological list of where the work has been exhibited; sales prices; description of the physical condition of the work; complete bibliography of the work and artist; notes on the subject matter, details on attributions, iconography, authenticity, etc.

WRITING FOR PUBLICATION

Although this handbook is intended primarily for the student, he may, particularly if he envisages a professional career in art history, be interested in some of the general practices of scholarly publication of articles. Publication is the means whereby the results of research can be put into the hands of interested people; as such, it is a mechanical extension of the research paper, but to the beginner it is usually a mysterious world to which access seems difficult and obstructed by unknown passwords and Open Sesames.

Because art history and its historians cover such a vast amount of cultural territory, the results of an art historian's studies may appear not only in journals devoted to the history of art but also in those concerned with archaeology, criticism, social studies, history, esthetics, Americana, or Orientalia. Because of this diversity of journals, these remarks on publication practices should be considered as generally true but also varying on minor points with the policies of particular journals.

The Journal and its Editor. Scholarly journals are published as a service to the students of a discipline, usually by professional societies, or sometimes by university presses, institutes, or foundations. They rarely sell sufficient copies to pay for themselves, and, hence, usually operate under a gift or endowment or on a stipend provided by the sponsoring agency.

Editors of journals either receive no remuneration for their work or at most a small honorarium. A few salaried editors do exist, but they are so rare as not to be considered in a general discussion. Journal editors work at their task as a labor of love, a professional responsibility that carries some distinction and honor and a great deal of involvment in reading manuscripts, corresponding with authors, correcting and styling copy, dealing with printers, and arranging financing.

All reputable journals receive many times the number of manuscripts that they can possibly publish. Hence, all journals have a backlog of accepted manuscripts that will fill their publishing schedules for the next one to three years. Frustrating to the beginner, but quite expected by the experienced student, is a letter congratulating the author on the acceptance of his manuscript for publication with the notation that, because of the backlog of manuscripts held by the journal, the author may not see his article in print for perhaps as long as two years.

The reputation of the editor, the journal, and the society or publishing organization that sponsors the periodical depends upon the quality of the articles the journal contains. The editor bears the responsibility to see that only the best manuscripts he receives are printed. His concern is with the subject matter of the submitted manuscript, as well as with such matters as the conciseness of the presentation, the clarity of the writing and organization, the quality of the documentation, and the uniqueness of the contribution that the paper makes to the general body of art historical literature. He must also think of factors external to the quality of the paper, such as whether the article is appropriate to the interests and intellectual level of his readers, whether he has sufficient space to devote to a particularly long essay, whether he can afford the number of illustrations submitted, and whether the work required to get the manuscript into shape for publication is sufficiently merited by the contents.

These practical considerations of journal editing are mentioned only to stress the fact that editorial decisions by journals with good reputations in their fields are rarely capricious, arbitrary, or personal. The more important the journal, the more exacting its editorial policies. Some journals have a single editor who makes all decisions on rejection and acceptance of manuscripts. Many journals have an editorial board, whose members read manuscripts and make recommendations to the editor-in-chief. A single manuscript may have one or several readers, all of whom are volunteers, contributing their professional skills.

Submission of Manuscripts. Journals usually carry in each issue a "Note to Contributors" that provides information on how manuscripts should be submitted. Some journals occasionally publish a detailed account of manuscript specifications: how notes are to be arranged, standard abbreviations to be used, size and quality of photographs for reproduction, etc. Before submitting a manuscript for consideration, the author should consult the policy of the journal in question as printed in past issues. Unless otherwise stipulated, journals require only a single copy of a manuscript, but that must be the first (ribbon) typed copy rather than a carbon or photocopy. It is standard practice to require that all text, notes, and bibliography be typed double-spaced; to number notes serially and append them at the end of the text; to use only glossy photographic prints, preferably taken from the original work of art rather than copied; to have drawings done only in black-and-white line; and to have a separate listing of captions for all illustrations.

Students ask how perfect a manuscript should be before it is submitted. No amount of proofreading will guarantee that the paper is letter-perfect, but it is equally true that editorial boards are human: the less editorial work that needs to be done on a manuscript, the better the chances for publication. Obviously, the fact that a manuscript has an attractive format is not sufficient to insure publication, but a paper that is easy to read, neat in appearance, and put together with care and patience will earn it a careful reading by an editor. The same cannot be said for the dog-earred, scratched over papers with appended slips that too often come to the editorial desk. An author should remember that the editor and the international scholarly community of art historians will know and judge him by the amount of professional care he has expended upon his paper and its composition. An art historian should be especially aware of the visual impact of his written presentation.

It may be true that it is easier to place a short article than a long one, but that does not mean that only short articles should be written; rather, it means that an author should carefully and unrelentingly go over his manuscript, removing everything except that which is necessary to the argument he advances. It is an extremely rare author whose work cannot be shortened with profit. For example, a lengthy, interesting, but nonessential introduction to the main subject of a paper can usually be removed without harm to the topic and thereby can earn the author the gratitude of an editor who must economize on space.

Most articles are unsolicited, submitted for consideration by their authors; however, editors will also ask scholars whose work and reputation is familiar to them to submit an article. There is not much use writing an editor asking if he would like to see an article that one has written or contemplates composing. Unless the subject is completely unrelated to the material usually carried by the journal, the editor cannot know whether he wants the finished article for his journal without having read it. Probably no editor will commit himself or his journal until he has seen a completed manuscript. Time and fruitless correspondence will be saved if the author submits his article without preliminary negotiations. Authors should avoid sending a long letter accompanying a manuscript, explaining what the article attempts to prove, why it was written, what it accomplishes. If these matters are not crystal clear in the article itself, then the manuscript needs rewriting. Referees of an article are seldom influenced by the author's accompanying a manuscript with a letter listing his prior achievements.

An exact copy of a paper sent to any editor should be kept by the author. Manuscripts do get lost in the mails and between desks. Such occurrences are very infrequent, but most writers have had the experience at least once in their careers. Also, should the article be accepted for publication, the journal may not return the original manuscript with the galley proof that is to be checked against the author's writing.

Because journals are managed by scholars who have other professional duties which occupy their time, an author must practice patience in waiting to hear whether his manuscript has been accepted. However, a manuscript should never be submitted to more than one journal at a time; to do so is unprofessional.

The Rejected Manuscript. Because most scholarly editors run their journals in addition to their other professional duties, they and the members of their editorial boards are seldom able to write long discussions of rejected manuscripts to the authors. Sometimes manuscripts are returned with suggestions for revision. The editors may invite resubmission for consideration after revision. More usual is the short, polite note that says that the journal cannot accept the manuscript for publication.

It is natural for the author of a rejected manuscript to feel that the editor has erred in his judgment; indeed, he may have, but only the foolish writer will attempt to begin a debate by mail with an editor in an attempt, always vain, to convince the editor of his mistake. A general recommendation is that in the event that an intelligent eye has examined a paper and found it inadequate, the author should reexamine it himself with care and dispassion. If the essay stands up under such a close scrutiny, and the author still feels that he has said what he wants to say exactly as it should be said, then he should submit the manuscript to another journal. But, as a general rule, a rejection should be taken as a warning flag of the need for rethinking or rewriting.

There are many reasons for rejecting a manuscript, such as inadequate presentation, lack of originality, lack of coherence, insufficient documentation, too great a dependence on secondary sources, lack of significant contribution, duplication of other studies, inadequate coverage, and too generalized a topic for adequate handling. But a manuscript may be rejected for reasons not connected with the quality of the contents of the paper. For example, the essay, while excellent, may not be appropriate to the reader interest of a particular journal, or the manner of presentation may not be appropriate to the journal because it is too specialized or too generalized.

No matter what disappointment a rejection may bring, one should remember that editors rarely hold personal grudges, that their reasons are usually sound and spring from long experience, and that, in the long run, the rejection may encourage the writer to produce a better manuscript and save him the embarrassment a few years later of having his name attached to an article of which he is no longer proud.

The Accepted Manuscript. It is not unusual for a journal to take one to six months, and perhaps even longer, before notifying an author of acceptance or rejection. Each manuscript has to be logged in, given a quick inspection by the editor to determine if it is worth careful consideration, and, if so, whom he should ask to read it, mailed to the reader, returned to the editor, perhaps mailed to another reader and returned by him, reread by the editor along with the readers' commentaries, and then put into the routine of notifying the author of the journal's decision. Journals operate on minimal budgets and, hence, have a minimum of secretarial assistance; readers for journals are those scholars who are most busy with their own studies, which is the reason they have the professional competence to act as readers. Hence, everyone is short of time and must cram in manuscript reading when he can.

After an article is accepted, it may go to an editorial assistant who corrects minor errors of syntax, punctuation, notation, and infelicities of expression, and it may also be returned to the author for more drastic alterations or additions. The completed manuscript, with the editorial work finished, is then placed in the publishing schedule to be forwarded with other manuscript material for a single issue to the printer. Galley proofs are prepared by the printer, sent to the author to be corrected for typographical errors, and then checked again by the editorial office. The printer prepares page proofs from this corrected copy, which are rechecked by the editor, and then the final copy is sent to the printer for publication. Journals infrequently send the page proofs to the author for his correction; proofs on illustrations also are infrequently sent to the author, although some journals do follow the practice.

Reprints of Articles. Almost all journals provide the author with several separately bound reprints of his article without cost. Should the author desire additional copies, there are provisions for ordering them from the printer at the author's expense.

Payments to Authors. Professional and scholarly journals in the humanities normally do not pay authors for articles. Commercial journals and magazines contract for articles and pay for such writing. In some scholarly fields, particularly in some scientific areas, authors are not only unpaid but may be charged a per page fee for their accepted articles. In Europe, however, some scholarly publications in the arts pay a modest stipend to the author.

Journal Subscriptions. Must one be a subscriber to a journal, or a member of the society sponsoring the journal, to have an article considered for publication? Generally, being a subscriber or member does not seem to be a condition of publication.

Book Reviews. Most journals have book review editors who determine the books to be reviewed in the journal, obtain review copies from publishers, and place them in the hands of selected reviewers. It is a standard practice for journals to solicit reviews and not to accept voluntary reviews contributed without being requested.

Copyright on Articles. Normally copyright on an article is retained by the journal rather than by the author.

Illustrations for Articles. Permission to publish photographs of art objects and monuments must be obtained from the museum or collector supplying the photograph. If the author has taken the photograph himself, he still must obtain the permission of the owner of the art object photographed if he wants to publish it. Usually permission to use a photograph for scholarly purposes is freely given upon requests. Some private museums, collections, and photographers may charge a small fee, in addition to that charged for the photograph, for publication rights.

The author, not the journal, usually is responsible for obtaining the necessary permissions and paying any permission fees prior to publication. These permissions to use photographs may be obtained prior to placing an article with a journal, but many museums want to know where the photograph is to be published before granting permission. Hence, it is convenient to wait until an article is accepted before seeking permission. Most museums state the precise contents of the acknowledgment that must appear in print with the illustration. Because the registrars of museums maintain a record of the publication of their holdings, it is a courtesy to send them a reprint of the article.

The granting of permission to use a photograph extends for the single use for which the permission is requested. If the illustration is to be used a second time, permission must be obtained again. Some journals return the photographs to the author after the article has been to the printer, but some do not or will do so only on request.

Bernard Goldman is professor of art and art history at Wayne State University. He holds the Ph.D. degree from the University of Michigan (1959) and is the author of The Sacred Portal *(Detroit: Wayne State University Press, 1966).*

The manuscript was edited by Linda Grant. The book was designed by Gary Gore. The type face for the text is Photon Baskerville and the display face is also Baskerville.
The text is printed on Neutratext paper and the book is bound in Riegel's Carolina cover. Manufactured in the United States of America.